Overcoming the Software Crisis

Growing
Better Software

Marc Brevoort

Growing Better Software

Please support independent publishing.
This book is available through:
http://www.growingbettersoftware.com

Published by Marc Brevoort.

Special thanks go out to gallery.bufferchuck.net
and curator David De Groot.

Word processing performed on OpenOffice Writer.
Graphics made with the GNU Image Manipulation Program.
Running under GNU/Linux.

R7/81012

ISBN 978-0-9559824-0-8

Software is like a bonsai tree;
It needs planning, shaping,
pruning, dedication;
Skill and art go hand in hand.

Table of Contents

Introduction

Front matter

0.1 Acknowledgements

Thanks go out to all those who made this book possible. To my wife, who deserves more attention than she got during the process of writing this text; to my father, who introduced me to the digital world; to the many programmers who wrote the software used in putting together this text and provided it to the world for free; to those who share their programming knowledge online; and to all those who contributed their support to this text.

0.2 Preface

Over the years that I've worked as a programmer, to my surprise I have observed that many professional programmers have no formal education in computer science. One can only make guesses about the cause: Maybe it has always been this way, or perhaps it is the inevitable result of the burst .com bubble. In any case, source code is often of such poor quality that it is surprising that some systems work at all. It turns out there are no bad intentions involved. All the programmers that I know do the best they can, with the skills that they have.

The purpose of this text is to improve the quality of source code of computer programs by increasing awareness in programming by addressing common mistakes that occur over and over again.

To this end, this text provides techniques that can help to prevent and solve possible problems that occur when writing code. Additionally, this text may be used to troubleshoot existing systems and find out what could be done or what should have been done to get better results.

In the book Gulliver's Travels by Jonathan Swift[1], there was a war going on between 'Big Endians' and 'Small Endians' over the issue of whether a boiled egg should be broken on the big end or the small end. Obviously there are benefits and drawbacks to either way, and there may be no 'right' or 'wrong' way to do it. Similar heated discussions without 'right' or 'wrong' answers go on about various topics in programming; for instance, 'Big Endian' and 'Little Endian' byte ordering in fact borrowed its name from the aforementioned book.

---

1 See **Gullivers's Travels**, by Jonathan Swift (1667-1745), online at http://www.gutenberg.org/etext/829

After giving it some thought, I have deliberately decided not to avoid topics to which no absolute truth exists. As I intend to increase awareness in programming, I feel it is better to highlight the different sides of the story and let readers form their own opinion, than to keep these subjects untouched.

In many cases, the topics covered have impact far beyond written source code, but apply as strongly to other areas as well. To name an example: Version control clearly does not apply only to source code but also to written documents. Other examples include initialization, preventing duplicate efforts, and so on. When using this text, the programmer should be aware that topics may be broader than writing source code, and seek other situations where the same principles might apply.

I have tried to keep this text simple enough to be used by average programmers, but even experienced programmers may still learn a thing or two from this text.

This text does not pretend to have the ultimate answer to all programming issues, but addresses common problems to make programmers aware of the trouble that frequently observed programming styles may cause. By increasing this awareness and providing alternatives to problematic programming style, I hope to provide guidelines that will help improve the average quality of source code.

0.3 About the author

Over two decades ago, I started programming computers in BASIC, which was the main programming language of home computers at the time. I've been writing commercial software for around fifteen years, of which around a decade professionally. I have programmed in a wide range of programming languages, ranging from low-level languages such as assembly, to high level languages such as Java, Perl, PHP and C# and just about everything in between. I have also played around with a few rather exotic languages such as Forth and Miranda, which influenced my programming style for the better, although I've never used those languages for anything serious. Over the years, I have developed anti-virus software, file system tools, audio processors, various interpreters, copy protection schemes, cross-assemblers, device drivers and content management systems, as well as business automation and workflow software.

I realize this does not make me an authority on the subject of programming. However, I feel that after decades, I do have some knowledge that is worth sharing. I've learned mostly by reading publications and books by others; Now that I've found the time to put together these pages, I hope they will give back a bit and help make the programming world a better place.

0.4 About the examples in this text

This text contains snippets of source code intended to illustrate the situations being discussed. These situations are generally not bound to any programming language in particular. For this reason, the source code for most examples in this text is written in a fictional programming language.

This fictional language will show strong similarities with a large number of modern, imperative programming languages such as C, C++, Java and C#. One should however not expect that code in this text actually compiles or runs on any of these platforms; the code is merely intended to illustrate a point. The principles shown should apply to most programming languages out there.

Over the years, programming languages have been extended with many useful features, such as object-orientation and exception handling. These are useful tools that the programmer has available to let the code work as intended. However, the techniques discussed in this text generally are intended to be independent of programming language. It is possible to write object-oriented programs in machine language, as it is possible to simulate exception handling in BASIC (even the old-fashioned type, that still used line numbers). In this text the author attempts to view the syntax of a programming language and logic apart from each other. Programming languages are merely a means to express logic; this text attempts to order that logic.

0.5 Using this text

This text can be used in various ways. First of all, it is set up in such a way that you may read it, front to back.

As most topics are kept brief, you can also choose to read the topics that apply to you at that moment. Used in such a manner, this text may serve you as a reference.

You may have noticed that most chapter titles are set in an imperative tone. This will allow you to take the table of contents and use it to jog your memory while developing.

Finally, you may use the table of contents as a check list to troubleshoot your project.

Chapter 1

The roots of software

As the capabilities of computer hardware evolve, software systems are getting increasingly complex. This complexity becomes more and more difficult to manage. The result is a software crisis which has been going on for decades- where software is more often than not of poor quality. This poor quality is somehow accepted, by users and developers alike, albeit not without complaints- all too often 'the computer' is blamed when systems do not work as they should.

The only group of people on the planet capable of resolving these problems are software designers. Are we up to the task of keeping the most complex systems on the planet in good state?

1.1 The bonsai tree and the mighty oak

Once upon a time, two trees lived in a faraway land. One was a small bonsai tree; the other was a mighty oak. The bonsai was taken good care of by its master. Every now and then, its branches would be trimmed with delicate instruments, shaping it into a perfect work of art. The mighty oak proudly looked down upon the bonsai tree. "What good is a tree, if it won't provide a shelter from the sun?" it would say. "And what is up with all the spoiling?" After all, the mighty oak had grown there all on its own, without help, rooted firmly in the soil.

The pride of the oak was misplaced. Over the years, it had gathered quite a bit of moss and lost quite a few branches during thunderstorms. The oak didn't mind; it usually said that it didn't need those branches anyway, as it had so many of them. But it had stood there for so long in ever changing weather, that it had long started to rot from the inside. It was plagued with termites and other little bugs. Although magnificent at first sight, the oak was doomed.

At one dark night, there was another thunderstorm. A lightning bolt struck the old oak. The oak lost another branch, which fell on the house of the master of the bonsai tree. It took weeks to repair the damage. The old oak tree was considered a safety hazard and cut down. A big chainsaw cut through the rotten wood in seconds. A new acorn was planted. The bonsai tree didn't complain. It was being treated with even better care from that day on, as was the young oak.

The moral of this metaphorical story is that great software design doesn't happen overnight. Most systems 'happen' by lots of changes over a long period of time. This is understandable: the whole *point* of software is to be adaptable, in contrast to the hardware that it runs on.

Strangely, for a long time this fact has not been given due credit. Many computer science students have been taught to design systems by thinking of them as static designs, rather than as evolving systems[2]. Requirements would be collected, the system would be implemented and the project would be considered finished.

The benefit of this approach is that it allows us to precisely define when a system is considered finished. But in reality, we simply cannot foresee all future requirements of a system when we start working on it. As a result, we do not build the system all at once, but in phases. Each phase comes with its own set of requirements; new requirements often face as a result of how the system evolves.

Because of this, we could say that complex software is never statically designed, but grown. The result often feels quite organic indeed, and may grow out of our control unless we take proper care of our systems. Only systems that are taken proper care of will be a joy to maintain.

---

2 Fortunately, the ever-changing nature of software is starting to gain the recognition that it deserves. Agile development methods are now being taught in most courses.

1.2 What makes a good programmer?

*In air travel, a good landing is one from which
you can walk away.*

*A great landing is one after which
the airplane can be reused.*

A good programmer is a programmer that gets the job done. A problem arises, it is analyzed, a solution is implemented and the problem is solved.

As it turns out, what is commonly considered 'getting the job done' is not even half the work. Around three quarters of all programming hours spent are in maintenance activities[3]. A great programmer is aware of this, and designs software in such a way that the burden of maintenance is eased. As it turns out, great programmers can be ten times as productive as 'journeyman programmers' - and they're a bargain, because their salary is rarely proportional to the time they save.

Maintenance activities involve, mainly:

- Fixing bugs and other issues that may still arise as the system is used

- Updating the system (and documentation, etc.) to reflect the latest requirements and insights

---

3   See **The Magic Cauldron**, online at
    http://www.catb.org/~esr/writings/cathedral-bazaar/magic-cauldron/

The easier a programmer makes it to perform maintenance on a program, the better that program is. This is not to say that when a programmer has built a maintenance-free system, it automatically makes him or her a great programmer.

The system may have been delivered a year after the deadline. Or it may have cost ten times the intended budget. The programmer may be a first class jerk, claiming all requested features are 'impossible' to implement - leaving the customer with a useless system.

A great programmer is not only able to deliver a low-maintenance system, but also able to deliver it on time and within budget - while staying friendly to the customer and providing added value to their business.

1.3 Say goodbye to absolute truths

In creating software, we are faced with some principles based on formal, classical theory. Some of these principles are: Normalize your data structures, communicate, follow procedures to guarantee software quality. These are indeed all best practices.

We should not abandon these, nor take them too far. It doesn't require explanation that abandoning best practices altogether is a bad idea. But taking best practices too far may also harm our project. We may get stuck over-analyzing a problem, be in endless meetings to discuss changes and be hindered by the bureaucracy of formal procedures.

There are situations where opposing perspectives exist on how to best deal with certain issues. People tend to think that if one of these perspectives is right, the opposing one must be wrong. This is a misconception; we should not always think in terms of 'right' or 'wrong'. Sometimes the perspectives are simply different.

This text deals with a few of such situations, neither of which is always right or always wrong. I will try to highlight the drawbacks and benefits of either side, when I can. When dealing with these topics, please consider both perspectives, whenever applicable. After careful consideration, choose the one that best suits your purposes.

1.4 Fix your development process

Often, the software development process is defined as something like this:

1. Coding (new features)

2. Testing

3. Fixing bugs

4. Delivering the project

5. Cleaning up code

6. Writing documentation

The last two steps (after delivering the project) fall in the "We'll do that later" category, which we might as well call the "We're not going to do that" category, because usually the next development cycle starts as soon as a project is delivered. As a result, there is no time to clean up the code or to write documentation. The lack of cleaning up code in turn causes more bugs, which in turn leaves even less time for the "We'll do that later" steps. In other words, the above development process is fundamentally broken.

The following revised development process addresses this problem. Documentation, code reading and testing have become an integral part of the development process, instead of being treated as overhead.

1. Writing documentation (specifically, producing a functional specification that is accepted by the client)

2. Designing and writing unit tests (see page 267)

3. Coding (new features) based on documentation

4. Building code and running unit tests. If any bugs were found, fix them and run unit tests again

5. Code reading (by another team member)/cleaning up code. If any changes were made, go back to step 4

6. Perform peer reviews against functional specification: Let another team member test your code. If any bugs were found, fix bugs and go back to step 4

7. Nightly build

8. Regression tests. If any bugs were found, fix bugs and go back to step 4

9. Integrating partial documentation with the master document

10. Delivering the project along with the documentation

When our team adapted this process, the defect rate of our software dropped dramatically. The first sign of this was that the client started reporting mostly old defects (from previous releases) rather than new defects. At some point, old defects stopped coming in, which in turn freed up some time for some long overdue code cleaning. In effect, the extra steps made our development process more efficient.

By working according to a documented development process, all team members will know what is expected from them at what time. This helps ensure proper communication at critical moments. New developers that join the team will be able to get up to speed quickly.

Implementing a new development process takes time, but peer reviews and code reading can be introduced by simply deciding to. Take in account that programmers can be sensitive about their code. There is a risk that some team members will feel personally attacked by code reading sessions. Because of this, we must describe and agree on which coding practices are acceptable and which ones are not. Issues not described should not be part of the formal evaluation, although they may be chalked up for inclusion at a later stage.

Before you start peer reviews or code reading sessions, make sure you can track the number of defects, so that your team can ask for a raise once the defect rate drops.

1.5 Stay up to date, strategically

As programmers, we continuously need to invest in learning new things to keep up with the state of technology. As we are mere mortals, we can not possibly learn everything there is to know at the rate that things are developing. We have to make choices to get to the skill set that best serves us.

In choosing what skills to develop, you may find the following criteria useful:

- What are your knowledge gaps?

- What are your interests?

- What skills are in demand?

- How durable do you want your skills to be?

- Do you want to specialize in a certain subject or broaden your horizon?

After having programmed in assembly language for a few years, I found that those skills proved not to be very durable. It was quite an effort just to keep up to date, as hardware was evolving rapidly. Also, I found that programming in assembly very much limited me to writing code just for the processor and platform that I happened to work on at the time.

If marketability of your knowledge is important to you, you can either choose to specialize in a subject that very few people know about, or go with the latest hypes. Be prepared however, that if you follow the latest hype, the bubble may burst and you may find yourself unmarketable.

If you keep a toolbox or set of libraries, and you don't want to keep rewriting it from scratch over and over again, durability of your knowledge may be more important to you. In general, technologies that have been adapted to various platforms and operating systems are more resistant to ageing than vendor-specific technologies. Also, standardized technologies are often a strong base to learn to work with vendor-specific ones. Thus the emphasis of this text on writing portable code; If you can write cross-platform software, most likely you have adapted a more durable skill set than someone who only follows the latest hype, or who develops only for one specific platform or operating system.

A good exercise to write proper software is to port over a piece of software from one platform several others, each time porting the last port to the next platform. When done right, after each port, your code will tend to contain less platform-specific code. In the process, you will probably pick up a few platform-specific skills, which will likely be key skills for that platform. These key skills will serve you well when at some point you need to target that specific platform.

1.6 Learn from the masters

We normally do not hear the names of programmers in the daily news. As it seems, most programmers usually keep a low profile. However, there are quite a few masters that have earned respect and a worldwide reputation by their efforts. To name a few:

- Richard M. Stallman, founder of the GNU project;

- Linus Torvalds, creator of the Linux kernel;

- Brian W. Kernighan and Dennis M. Ritchie, inventors of the C programming language;

- Larry Wall, creator of the Perl programming language;

- Andrew S. Tanenbaum, creator of the Minix operating system;

- Donald Knuth, author of The Art of Programming.

There are many more that deserve a place in the above list, but space is limited. If you didn't make it into the list - better luck next time.

In any case, many master programmers have made the source code of their life's work available online. Your favourite search engine will take you there, and will allow you to learn a thing or two from their code.

Chapter 2

Communication

Except for projects that are carried out only for and by the same individual, we will have to deal with other people when developing software: our bosses, our co-workers, the client, our users.

Communication - especially proactive communication - is a key skill in this. Effective communication works in two directions: It will help us understand what is expected from us, and it will help the others understand what they are going to get. By communicating about a system, the client will feel involved in its design and more readily accept it. It greatly increases the chances that a project will be successful, and should it project fail with flying colours, at least it will be obvious why.

2.1 Split technical from functional issues

We may perform an information analysis with or without discussing a system-to-be with anyone. The guideline for deciding between discussing the system with someone else or not is very simple; if there is a client involved, we must discuss the system with that client. The word 'client' is used in the broad sense of the word; the client may well be your employer.

The initial talk with a client to discuss a system should be simple enough; it is intended to give a broad overview about what it is that we are going to build. In any project, if we are to keep grip on a project, we should separate functional concerns from technical concerns from the beginning on. Functional matters can be identified by asking *what*: "What problem are we trying to solve?" Technical issues can be identified by asking *how* : "How are we going to solve the problem?"

As projects get discussed in more and more detail, the boundaries between 'what' and 'how' will become more vague. We may have to tell 'no' to the client. When a client says "We want a button that does this or that", what is the problem that the client wants to solve? Surely the problem is not to add a button. Adding a button is *how* the client envisions solving the problem. However, a button may not be the best way to solve the problem. We were hired for our expertise, it is all right to subtly stop the client from telling us how to do our job.

Of course, blurting out "Don't tell me how to do my job, am I telling you how to do yours?" won't help. Our client will be offended. Instead, you can ask, "What is the problem you are trying to address by adding a button?" and suggest, for example, that a drop-down box may be a better choice to address the problem, if you think this is the case.

Keep in mind that the client is the functional designer of the system; we are to stay in charge of technical decisions. These technical decisions also include the platform or programming language in which the problem is to be solved.

2.2 Prefer written communication

It is in human nature to try to get the best possible deal, and then to try to push things a bit further. When dealing with clients, this can be a source of stress to both sides. During a coffee break (or over a nice cup of tea, if you're British), a client may ask for a little something extra, we say "sure" and before we know it we find ourselves trapped in an endless project, with heavily increased maintenance.

We shouldn't assume that the client will take care of documentation for us, as the informal talk is beneficial to them: the added functionality is off the record, but it will be built in anyway, most likely at our personal expense.

Should the 'little something extra' contain a bug, the client will rightfully insist on having it fixed. The more little extras we provide, the bigger the amount of time that needs to be spent off the record.

We can protect ourselves from this in two ways: by keeping things formal or by simply saying no. Clients like to hear yes, so generally we will keep things formal. This doesn't mean writing a full fledged design document for every little extra, but the least we can do is keeping a record, for instance by confirming the functionality by email. A few lines is enough, as the following short example will show.

Dear Client,

We discussed adding a menu choice 'Save All' intended to save all open files instead of just the current one.

This menu choice will be built in as soon as this email is confirmed by a responsible manager.

Best regards,

Programmer Bob

By having a written record of the requested new functionality, we create the possibility of charging for it.

Still, sometimes it is better to say no. At some point, I was at a client to rescue a project which was months overdue because of a batch process that was troubled by bugs. Halfway the first day of debugging, the client asked if I could add an extra view to the database: "It will only take you ten minutes". Obviously, adding functionality to an already late project which I was supposed to rescue wasn't why I was there. I tactfully told them that that wasn't why I was there, but that I'd consider it if there was any time left by the end of the day.

As it turned out, the system was in worse state than expected. After four days of working overtime, everything was finally working the way it should. The next Monday, the project was finally taken into production. The rescue operation was considered a success. The extra view was never implemented.

Documentation also helps communication. At some point, our team spent several weeks writing an official functional design document for a complex system of a client. A few hundred pages of condensed documentation were produced. We didn't think the client would ever pick up the documentation and read it, but at least it was paid work.

What happened next was unexpected. The functional documentation became a central tool in filing bug reports, and to distinguish between bug reports and feature requests. We got comments such as "According to paragraph N, the system should raise an error message in these conditions, but it doesn't". and "The system raises an error message and the documentation mentions that it should, but a non-blocking warning message would be enough. Would you give an estimate needed for this change?"

Ever since we started seriously documenting the system, the documentation was considered a requirement to maintain software quality. It made expectations clear to both parties involved.

2.3 Determine limitations

During the phase in which we are discussing a system with a client, it is important to know which measurable standards the system should live up to. We should make sure the limitations of our system are known by both parties involved, objective and realistic. Important to consider are for example:

- How much data must the system be able to handle?

- How many users should the system be able to serve simultaneously?

- How much scheduled/unscheduled downtime is allowed?

- How fast should the system respond?

- How many bugs is it allowed to have?

- When should it be delivered?

- How much is the system allowed to cost?

- What software (and which versions) is needed by our system?

- What are the specifications of the hardware will be used to run the system on?

  - How much drive space will be available?

  - How much network bandwidth will be available?

  - How much RAM?

  - What screen resolution (or range of screen resolutions) do we need to support?

The list above is still incomplete, so you can extend it as needed. Needless to say, there is quite a difference between the complexity of a birthday calendar application of a start-up company, and a governmental tax database containing data of the entire population of a country. Likewise, the correctness of an air traffic control system is usually more critical than that of a program that plays tic-tac-toe or a nice game of chess.

It should be obvious that certain combinations of limitations in writing software are mutually exclusive. If our client demands such combinations, it will make it highly unlikely that our project will succeed. There is a saying that goes around in various incarnations:

Cheap, good, fast - choose any two

This should be kept in mind at all times when discussing system limitations with our client. Based on the demands the client makes, we can make some demands ourselves.

2.4 Give the client some responsibility

While building a system for a client, we will often run into little details that could not have been foreseen. We may often come to a solution with a bit of creativity, when there are no big, obvious deviations from the original project specification. In many cases however, it is a good idea to consult the client. This will prevent the client from being overwhelmed with a large number of small surprises in a later stage.

Unfortunately, we can not always count on the availability of our client. If our client is not available for comments, we may get ourselves in trouble. We may decide on a solution that we think is best, while our client may have preferred the other solution. Either way, we may be wasting time on implementing a wrong solution.

The more little assumptions we make, the greater is the chance that at some point we deviate from the wishes of the client. At the very least, this will make the client less accepting of the final result.

Because of this, it is vital that the client is given some responsibility for the outcome of the project. Customers do not always have to be around while we are developing and designing for them; often a one-minute phone call or lunch break talk can clear up a lot. In any case, our clients should be aware that their availability and choices can greatly influence the outcome of a project. This isn't a bad thing; it will increase their feeling of involvement for the project, which will help during the acceptance phase.

Things don't always go our way. In the past I've heard clients ask for features that would cause their project to get into big trouble. In some cases, these clients could be brought to their senses by explaining what the implications would be: "I could build this feature, but it would cause the system to break. It won't be in your best interest".

In other cases, I've heard customers insist on features that would break their system, even after they were warned about the implications. Invariably, this was the result of political games. So, the features were implemented and the system broke down. At least the responsibilities were clearly defined.

In short, our customer is part of our team and should be available for comments. This will help prevent a project from getting stuck and will help its acceptance. Be sure to be aware of the risk involved, which is that some clients like to change their mind all the time. Written communication will help address this risk.

2.5 Work from complete specifications

Many a programmer has sighed, "Clients don't know what they want". We build something, and when we show it to the client, it's back to the drawing board. This has nothing to do with the natural growth or evolution of the system, but with incomplete or wrong specifications for part of the system. We must make sure the functional specifications are sufficiently complete and well understood by all parties before starting to implement something. It is our job to help our clients figure out what they want.

When clients say "I want to be able to choose the name from a list", they probably do not realize the implications that this may have. Where does the list come from? Who maintains it? Do we need to create a maintenance module for the list too? What about access control for this module?

Then we need to deal with the question 'how many' and with constraints: How many names are there in the list - ten, one hundred, millions? What if there are no names in the list? What if there is only one name in the list, should it be preselected or should the default be empty to prevent mistakes? Is it obligatory to choose a name from the list? Can multiple names be selected? What if the desired name is not (yet) in the list?

All these questions and more will influence the design decisions that need to be made to answer to the wishes of the client. They will also influence the time needed to implement the result. Clients who are aware of these questions will also be aware that it takes time to make a system that suits their needs.

2.6 Help your client choose what's best

To clients, the ideal solution is the solution that best serves their needs. Once, I had a client with employees performing surveys throughout the country. The results were to be sent back to main office on a daily basis, to be published on a website. The employees had laptops at their disposal, with modem internet access. Manually entering the results online via a slow modem connection proved impractical, and at hotel phone rates, quite expensive. A program specifically aimed at entering and sending the data was estimated to take a week to develop. Deploying such a program to the laptops that were always on the move was perceived as an issue. The website ran on Linux with Apache, whereas the laptops ran Windows.

The solution proved simple and effective. The client turned out to be relatively proficient in creating spreadsheets. With only a slight bit of assistance, he managed to create a spreadsheet that accepted and validated survey data. The spreadsheet was exported to a delimited text file. These text files could be uploaded to the server in seconds, solving the problem of the high phone bills. In one day of work, an import module was created for the web server to accept and validate files. To receive data from the notebooks, the web server would have needed an extension anyway, so no additional work was needed here. The import module was pretty picky about what it considered valid data; only completely valid files were accepted. In case of trouble, a clear log explained exactly what went wrong.

The client only specified what the problem was (high hotel phone bills) and wanted a solution for that. The solution initially suggested by the client was a separate application, which would have taken considerably longer to implement, even without considering roll-out.

The client was open to alternative solutions. The spreadsheet solution was realistic, took less time to implement, and most of the work could be done by the client himself. A bit of training to the users proved to go a long way for this client, who was on a low budget.

Should a separate application have been built, the time needed for return-on-investment would have been considerably longer. In this case, development time had been cut drastically. In addition, the solution had some benefits:

- Would updates be needed to the spreadsheet, the client could perform these himself.

- The spreadsheets were exported and sent as plain text. This not only cut the transfer time, but also eliminated the dependency on a specific spreadsheet format. The result is more flexibility: should the client decide to change from one spreadsheet program to another, or to have an application developed to send the data, the file format can be maintained.

- The solution provided useful functional redundancy: If directly uploading the data would fail for some reason, sending the spreadsheet files by e-mail was a realistic alternative.

2.7 Prototype on paper

When we are as lucky as to design a system from scratch, especially in its early stages, a lot of input from the client is needed to provide the best match between our technology and their wishes. Providing a prototype in this stage greatly aids communication. Unfortunately, there is a risk when providing the client with a coded example: it is easily confused for the real thing, and the client may grow impatient waiting for the final version. After all, in the first week of the project the system was already almost done, wasn't it?

To prevent this confusion, I find it helpful to draw the earliest draft of the prototype on paper, rather than showing a model on screen. Before writing a single line of code, this allows me to visually show what happens when a button is clicked, and feedback from the client can immediately be taken into consideration. By making careful notes, a rather precise model can already be made at this stage, and the notes double as documentation. This paper prototype serves as basis for a functional design document (put together with a word processor) which basically outlines how the system should react under all circumstances. Once this document is ready, we pretty much already have a user manual for the system, which doubles as a functional design document. There will be little room for confusion about the scope of the project: Whatever is not in the documentation was outside the scope of the project.

Alternatively, if you're handy with computer graphics, you may be able to draw a quick mock-up of what the system will look like. Especially changes in existing user interfaces can be drawn quickly, as a screen shot may serve as basis for the picture.

For communication purposes, it is no problem if a few user interface elements are a few pixels off; this will in fact help the user distinguish between our prototype and the finished product.

Another approach is to let the users create a paper prototype themselves. This will take you straight into their world, which will help you understand their perspective on things. The involvement of the users will help their acceptance and the usability of the system.

Keep in mind, however, that your users may not see the technical implications of the system that they're proposing. You may need to adjust their prototype to make it realistic.

2.8 Share your knowledge

Show your code to fellow programmers and explain it to them. This will automatically make it easier for them to maintain your code, should it at some point be necessary.

It will also stimulate your co-workers to give comments on the code. When a co-worker asks you "Why are you doing that in this-or-that way?" or "Have you thought of ...", this either gives you a chance to improve your code or their skills.

Knowledge may also be shared by means of code reviews. Other ways are by making documentation available in a known spot (a public share, version control system or a wiki), by creating a forum, mailing list, knowledge base or otherwise.

Chapter 3

Software Architecture

A key issue that distinguishes great programmers from average programmers is the architecture of their software systems. A system that has a solid architecture will take less effort to maintain and extend. This chapter discusses the cornerstone of proper system architecture: information analysis. Information analysis deals with the structure of information. A proper understanding of information analysis will help us keep our information and our systems structured, making it a lot easier to develop low-maintenance systems. Lack of understanding is almost a guarantee for chaotic, high-maintenance systems.

3.1 What is information analysis?

Information analysis is the practice of obtaining information about information (which is also called meta-information), usually with the primary goal of designing a database or data structure capable of effectively storing the given information. A secondary goal is to provide enough flexibility to allow us to enhance the application later on, which is essential for the healthy growth of a system. Usually, information analysts represent the relationship between bits of information by means of diagrams. Commonly used methods are:

- ERD (Entity Relationship Diagrams)

- NIAM (Nijssens Information Analysis Method, later renamed Natural-language Information Analysis Method); which evolved into

- ORM (Object-Role modelling)

- FCO-IM (Fully Communication-Oriented Information Modelling)

These methods serve mostly the same purpose. Their specific details are beyond the scope of this text, but we will briefly discuss the underlying concept.

It is commonly understood that information analysis needs to be performed when designing databases and data structures. As our code needs to deal with the data structures that it uses (be it databases or otherwise), it is directly influenced by the quality of the information analysis, as will be shown briefly.

In its simplest form, an information analysis describes only relationships between things. This is done in terms of 0, 1 and many. This is reflected in our code as follows:

- The number 0 usually implies that we need to perform a validation for the existence or absence of a relationship: "If the person does not have an email-address, do not attempt to send mail there".

- The number 1 usually implies a relationship between different types of data, and thus our system will contain code to handle that relationship.

- The number 'many' usually implies the presence of multiple relationships; for instance, a person can have many phone numbers. In code, this general case is normally solved by means of a loop.

3.2 Beware of N instead of many

All diagrams in the world won't prevent us from solving problems for a fixed number of entities, rather than for 'many' of them. This is a common mistake, which we should be aware of when designing a system.

This mistake manifests itself in data structures that have several fields or properties that represent essentially the same type of information, for instance:

```
class person
{
    date birthdate;
    string name;
    person child1;
    person child2;
    person child3; /* fixed maximum of 3
                       children */
}
```

We can't iterate these properties with a loop[4]; this means we will need to write several pieces of code, one to deal with each property. Changes in one piece of code imply the others need to be updated as well. In other words, solving a problem for a fixed number of entities rather than 1 or many will increase maintenance. It also creates an unnecessary logical limitation in our system.

---

4   Some object-oriented languages provide a workaround by allowing access to Run-Time Type Information. This will however disallow us to find certain problems as early as in compile time.

The following example has basically the same problem, although it is slightly less obvious, and as such much more common:

```
class person
{
    date birthdate;
    string name;
    phone phoneHome;
    phone phoneOffice;
    phone phoneCell;
}
```

When several such mistakes meet, our metaphorical bonsai tree soon turns into an old, rotten oak: we must write code for all permutations of the mistakes, and maintenance will quickly get out of hand[5]. Additionally, data structures designed for N instead of 'many' are sensitive to design changes. The following solves this, and once again allows us to loop through the list of children or phone numbers.

```
class person
{
    date birthdate;
    string name;
    person [] child; /* array of (many)
                        children */
}
```

---

5   If the phone fields are all merely informative, only intended to provide information to humans and never used by the system itself for automation purposes, we can actually get away with this. But we can not predict what the system will look like in the future, so why should we take the risk?

The case of the various types of phone numbers is solved in a similar manner. By defining the various types of phone number as enumeration, their proper usage in code can be checked in compile time.

```
type phone
{
    enum numbertype=(Home, Office, Cell);
    string number;
}


class person
{
    date birthdate;
    string name;
    phone [] phonenumber; /* array of (many)
                             phone numbers */
}
```

Another benefit from this "many instead of N" approach is that it also helps prevent users from abusing fields for the wrong purpose: If a client has several cell phones and no home phone, we can allow our users to select the correct type of phone number, rather than forcing them to enter a cell phone number in a home phone or fax number field.

When these fields are for use by human operators only, this may not be a problem. However, if at some point we want to extend our system with faxing functionality, it would be very convenient if the "fax number" field on screen actually contains a fax number. A proper design will help us prevent such database pollution.

3.3 A rudimentary information analysis

In this paragraph, I'll show that at least a rudimentary information analysis does not have to be a big effort. No fancy tools or diagrams are required.[6] Let us take a look at a simplified example, the information analysis of a book (which, as it happens, is a pretty good read).

```
Writing Solid Code
Author: Steve Maguire
ISBN: 1556155514
```

What can we say about the above book? First of all, the above information is not complete. If we would be computers, we would not know what the first line of the above example would represent. Speaking as humans, we actually do not know this either. We can say that the book is 'Writing Solid Code', which is not entirely accurate. It is more accurate to say that the *title* of the book is 'Writing Solid Code'. The name of the author is Steve Maguire, and the book has an ISBN (international standard book number) which is 1556155514.

Let us proceed by making statements about the intended book. Ideally, in a proper information analysis, these statements are facts about the real world. In any case, the statements will represent the inner working of our system. The closer the model of our system matches the real world, the less maintenance we will be able to expect in the future.

---

6 It may not be worth it to spend a lot of time on drawing diagrams, unless they are considered essential for communication, or if your client loves to see pictures.

So, here we go:

```
Each book must have at least one title.
Each book can have at most one title.
Each book must have at least one author.
Each book can have many authors.
Each book must have at least one ISBN.
Each book can have at most one ISBN.
Each book is identified by its ISBN.

Each author must have at least one name.
Each author has at most one name.
Each author is identified by its name.
```

When we read the above sentences backwards, we hopefully won't find any satanic messages, but we will be able to gain even more information about the system.

```
Each title must belong to a book
Each title can belong to several books

Each author can write many books
Each author must have (written) one or
                                    more books

Each ISBN must belong to at least one book
Each ISBN must belong to at most one book

Each name belongs to at least one author
Each name can belong to at most one author
```

Are there any incorrect assumptions in the above? Sure there are. That is the whole point about performing an information analysis: We try to find facts. As such, it is our job to prove the above rules wrong. This is most easily done in the second part we just wrote down, for example:

Each title must belong to a book

This statement may be true in a certain system. But not all titles in the world belong to books. Some titles may belong to songs, movies, paintings or albums. If our system may contain all of these, it is more accurate to call them medium-titles rather than simply titles. If our system will contain only books, perhaps it is better to call our titles book-titles. This explicitly expresses to our client what we are talking about.

Each title can belong to several books

This is definitely true. Perhaps also to other media, but we are leaving this out of consideration for now. But the fact that a title can belong to several books is without question.

Each author must have (written) one or more books

This is also true- otherwise the person wouldn't be an author, but merely a person. By saying this, we introduce another type of information: people. A person can write a book or not, and this decides whether he or she is a (book)author or not. In other words,

Each author is a person

What do we know about a person? We could say that a person is an author that has not written any books. But as in information analysis we like to speak in general truths, we like to use the word each. So, it would be more accurate to say that each author is a person that has written one or more books. In a sense, authors are a specialized subset of the total group of people. Now that we see this, we should make sure which rules that apply to authors also apply to people.

```
Each author must have at least one name.
Each author can have at most one name.
Each author is identified by his/her name.
```

Well, this seems to apply to people more than it applies to authors. It's wrong too. Several people can have the same name, so a name alone isn't suitable as identifier. We should find a better way to identify people.

```
Each person must have at least one name.
Each person can have at most one name.
Each person must have at least one
                    national insurance number.
Each person can have at most one
                    national insurance number.
Each person is identified by his/her
                    national insurance number.
```

If now we say "Each author is a person", this automatically implies that each author also has a name, and a national insurance number that can be used to identify that author.

For those who are into object-oriented programming, this should ring a bell: this is inheritance. An author is everything that a person is, plus he or she has written a book (or other medium)[7]. For simplicity, in this initial version of the system, an author is exactly one person. Let us continue:

```
Each author can write many books.
Each ISBN must belong to at least one book.
Each ISBN must belong to at most one book.
```

7　Perhaps artificial intelligence at some point will bring us computer authors. An author list would then need to include both types of author. In object-oriented programming, this possibility of treating different data types as the same thing is known as polymorphism.

All these statements are true.

Each name belongs to at least one author

This one is tricky. I'll say this is false, because a name does not have to belong to an author- it can belong to non-author entities. Specifically, after saying that an author is a person, it is more correct to say that a name belongs to a person rather than to the author. It would then also be clearer to speak of a person-name. A specific author-name exists too: It is called a pseudonym. We could add it to our information analysis if we want, but let us not over-complicate for now.

Each name can belong to at most one author

We have previously proved this to be false – first of all, a name does not belong to an author but to a person: In a sense, a person can be considered the 'base class' of an author.

Second, there can be several people with the same name. Thus the talk about the national insurance number earlier.

We now have performed the major part of the information analysis by writing down general truths by using the word *Each*.

We have answered some important questions:

- How much minimum?

- How much maximum?

- Are there obligations?

- Do these obligations lead to sub-types?

- By what property can we identify each entity?

Other questions to answer are:

- Are there any exclusions?

- Is all the information in the system explicit?

- Is any information duplicated in the system?

If people are divided into subtypes 'good guys' and 'bad guys', then if a person would be a 'bad guy', this would automatically exclude that person from the 'good guys'. When the system explicitly contains all information that it needs, we no longer need to rely on implicit information (such as, in the beginning of this chapter, that 'Writing Solid Code' is actually the title of a book) and assumptions that may turn out to be wrong. For all we know, 'Writing Solid Code' could have been the tip of the day.

It should be noted that for maintainability purposes of a system, we should make an information analysis based on only three numbers: 0, 1 and many. If something is 'more than one', we have to take in account the case of 'many', otherwise we will create unnecessary logical limitations in our system.

The most obvious place where we will see this is in the design of databases, but the same happens in code. The results of this will be discussed in the next paragraphs.

3.4 A recipe for disaster

Let us imagine a library that used to order exactly one copy of any book. To better serve their readers, the library wanted to have several copies of some books. The ISBN that was formerly used as identifier for each book was not unique enough anymore, because each copy of the book would have the same code, so it wouldn't be possible to identify exactly which copy of a book had not been returned.

To solve this, the in-house programmer of the library appended a digit to the ISBN, which was used as library book number. This, as it turned out, was the start of a lot of chaos. The system got a lot slower, but still worked fine otherwise. The first problem arose when the library ordered a dozen copies of a best-seller. After all, a single digit only warranted a maximum of 10 books with a given ISBN. "No problem", assured the programmer, "I'll just append another digit."

All code that isolated the sub-number of the book from the library book number had to be rewritten, which was quite a bit of work, because the identifier of library books was used all over the system. It turned out to be quite a task. The conversion of the database from 10+1 digits to 10+2 digits was the least. As it turned out, when a book was returned, it wasn't recognized because the bar code on the book only had 11 digits, while the new system used 12. The library staff didn't feel like sticking new bar codes on thousands of books. "No problem", assured the programmer again, "I'll just add a conversion table to the system". Meanwhile, the book exchange project between the city library and university library showed to have trouble dealing with the new codes as well. The old COBOL system that worked with fixed size ISAM records could not handle a sub-code of 2 digits.

The Dean mentioned how he already spent a considerable sum on the first sub-digit, and that the university didn't have the funds to justify altering the system again. "Oh well, we'll just allow them to exchange a maximum of 10 books then, they'll be able to use the old code then", said the programmer.

Needless to say, things got from bad to worse. Schedules slipped, the system got more and more troublesome to work with and after some time, conversion tables kept popping up, and finally the programmer got involved in a traffic accident. His successor couldn't figure out which of the now three different keys needed to be used when. The system was polluted with unnecessarily complexity, that was built in just to deal with wrong design decisions.

But what exactly is it that went wrong? The programmer overlooked the fact that information analysis also applies to itself. The average database management system is built around the assumption that

```
each entity is identified by at least 1 key
each entity is identified by at most 1 key
```

If instead we start using multiple keys, the information analysis of the information analysis is no longer correct. This means that the DBMS built on top of the previous assumption will no longer be able to assist us in these tasks. Suddenly we are on our own in solving the (theoretically infinitely big) problem of

```
each entity can be identified by many keys
```

But we never design systems like that, do we?

The fixed-length fields of the COBOL system of course also didn't help, as another logical restriction was imposed by the ISAM database. Had the data been exported to a delimited file or to an XML file, the problem would have been non-existent, as there would have been no hard length restriction on the field (save the maximum line length that some systems impose on text files).

There is something to say for using text files with fixed record length: it is fast. From a performance perspective, it may have been a sensible choice, but for data transfer it doesn't make a lot of sense.

From a maintenance perspective, using text files that work with fixed field length and fixed record length is asking for trouble, because field lengths keep changing, requiring us to change our import module over and over again.

This is to be expected: In the information analysis game of zero, one and many, using fixed field lengths is a typical "N instead of many" mistake. Using a delimited file works around this problem, because field lengths are no longer limited.

Also, in the above story, politics got in the way. As the Dean could not preview how many more times he would have to invest in an extra digit, he was unwilling to spend another bunch of money on something he thought was already done. Naturally - what would you do?

3.5 Preventing chaos

Of course the programmer in the previous story made more mistakes, most notably storing ISBN and book sequence number together in a single field, as library book key.

In information analysis, two equals many - if we store 'many' pieces of information in one field, it will no longer be possible to index by the individual bits of information in the field, which will impact performance. To solve this, we must have separate fields containing each snippet of information, and we can index our table once again.

However, we now see a table containing a compound key field (containing both ISBN and sequence number), followed by fields containing its individual components (one field containing the ISBN, the other field the sequence number). Should we base the key on its components, or the components on the key? The only correct answer is neither; they should be independent. This means that if the sequence number part of a book changes from 5 to 05 to allow for more copies of a book, the key should remain the same. This prevents the need for running a conversion.

Why not use a combination of fields as primary key? Because it would require you to use 'many' fields to identify a record. If you use 'many' fields to identify a record, and a field needs to be added, you need to change all code that identifies records of that type. If you use a single field as identifier, after a change it will still be a single field. In other words, the single-field key approach will save you maintenance.

Simply joining the values into a single compound key field doesn't work. Such keys are not suitable as permanent record identifiers, as they can be predicted to require changing every now and then.

Consider, for instance, a ten-digit product identification code: Two digits are assigned as country code, three digits as manufacturer code and the remaining five as manufacturer-specific product code. Soon, we will find that there are more than 100 countries, and we need an extra digit. Or a country has more than 1000 manufacturers, with the same result. Or two manufacturers merge, requiring the keys for half the product range to change.

Storing multiple types of information in an identifier will invariably cause us to run out of keys, or will require us to change keys. Forced maintenance is the result- a result that we were trying to prevent.

The fact that the keys may show some structure, makes room for another problem. It makes it easy to fall for the temptation of relying on implicit information: "Oh, this key already contains the country code, manufacturer code and product code, so I won't have to lookup that data anymore". This is a wrong assumption, as the product code in the key and the contents of the product code field do not have to be equal.

Using auto-incrementing numbers as keys for records causes a similar problem. First of all, we cannot safely use auto-numbers on a decentralized, distributed system. Is this a big deal? Perhaps not, if you're fine with a centralized system. Using auto-numbers does however mean that we almost immediately rule out the possibility of ever entering data off-site, from a laptop for instance, that has no connection to the server.

We could solve this by assigning a certain range of numbers to one system, and another range of numbers to another system, but at some point we will run out of numbers. If instead we interlace numbers, and for instance assign even numbers to one system and odd numbers to another, we forever limit ourselves to a fixed maximum number of systems- another unnecessary logical limitation. If the algorithm of assigning keys by auto-numbers is known, we will easily make the mistake of relying on implicit information: "Oh, this identifier falls in the 8000-9000 range so the record must have been created by this-and-that laptop". Later on, this reliance on implicit information may trap us into hard-coding these rules in our code, making it impossible to implement the same system for another client.

An effective way to solve these problems is to use keys that are structure-free and informationless. Something pseudo-random, yet guaranteed to be unique.

As there no longer is any implicit information in the identifiers, we will no longer be tempted to hard-code dependencies based on it. Why not simply start out on the right foot, and save ourselves the trouble of remodeling our system later on?

3.6 Use UUIDs where appropriate

The solution is as simple as it is effective. For identifying records, use exclusively keys that will forever be sufficiently large, such as UUIDs (Universally Unique Identifiers), also known as GUIDs (Globally Unique Identifiers)[8]. A UUID or GUID is a number or code which is guaranteed never to be generated twice, to a very high degree of certainty. Leading information analysts around the world have known this for a long time, and as such all major operating systems and DBMS software have GUID support. Even so, UUIDs or GUIDs are not quite as well-known as they should be, as auto-incrementing numbers die hard.

Usually, a UUID is represented as a series of hexadecimal characters (0-9, A-F). A long line of hex codes will not look very appealing to users. Because of this, it is recommendable to distinguish between a UUID and a user-key. A UUID will exclusively be used to maintain referential integrity within a database (or even across databases for that matter). The human-readable user-key is presented to the user.

For creating references between systems, it is recommended to use UUIDs as keys, exclusively. These are assigned only once, and you will never have to change them. No central authority is needed to generate UUIDs; because of this, they will work in decentralized, disconnected systems. Typical applications are off-line laptop use or interconnected databases.

As a general rule, never show the UUID to users. At some point, they will complain about whatever they see and demand you to change keys, which is exactly what we want to prevent. Instead, show the users a structured key- in our library example, we used ISBN plus sequence number as a user key.

---

8   See internet draft RFC 4122, ISO standard ISO/IEC 9834-8:2005

Should the user-key need converting (as in the case study before), the conversion will be limited to renaming the user-keys in a single table, as the referential integrity of our database is handled with the UUID keys. Inserting a zero in the user-key will have no consequences, because the user key isn't any more special than the title of the book; it has no impact on the referential integrity of the database. Whenever we need to display the user-key, we can look it up based on the UUID key.

Suddenly, exactly the same issue as before no longer has disastrous consequences. The link to the university system uses UUIDs and requires no more alterations. As the library marked the books with UUID bar codes as well, no maintenance to expect there either. Best of all, the library that just opened in the next city uses UUIDs as well. There will be no overlap between their identifiers and ours. Setting up a little book exchange program between the two would be nearly trivial. What a wonderful world.

One more tip: Most likely you will not have to implement your own UUID library. Depending on your DBMS, you may already have UUID or GUID functionality available: Under Oracle, it is implemented in function `SYS_GUID()`, MySQL supports `UUID()`, and PostgreSQL has a native UUID data type.

In a non-database context, UUIDS and GUIDs are available too. If you run Windows, your API already supports generating UUIDs - where did you think Dot-Net Class Ids came from? Under Linux, use `uuid_generate`.

Should you really need to implement your own UUID library, consult internet draft RFC 4122 for an example implementation.

Search the web for your options and rejoice.

3.7 Don't cut corners as systems evolve

This paragraph discusses a key factor in keeping systems maintainable. By applying this paragraph, you will make your job a lot easier. Please, take enough time to absorb this matter.

What happens when a system evolves? It changes, usually tending to get more complex. However, some changes are major, some are minor. What makes the difference between a major change and a minor one?

Generalizing, a major change is one where one of the following things happens:

- A 1-to-1 relationship between entities turns into a 1-to-many relationship

- A new type of entity is called into existence, which is to be a subtype of an existing type, other than at the 'edge' of the system.

In other words, in the game of 0, 1 and many, a relationship is promoted to the next level. Perhaps a person record is allowed to reference other person records to indicate a parent/child relationship between people. Perhaps the number of email addresses of a person increases, making it necessary to lookup the email address from another database table.

In case of a minor change, usually what happens is

- A constraint is added to the system

- A new entity or entity-type is added as a leaf or node, on the 'edge' of the system

In other words, a limitation is added to the system, or whatever is added has no big impact on the functioning of the system- it may in fact simplify it. Perhaps a description field is added to a person record, which is just used as memo field for the users (but which has no functional implications otherwise).

What we often see happen is the following mistake: An 1-to-1 relationship should be turned into a 1-to-many relationship (a major change), but instead in turned into a 1-to-N relationship (as if it is a minor change). As a result of an attempt to keep the data structure simple, our code will get a factor N more complex, instead of a factor 1. A lot of code duplication and added maintenance is the result.

What happens is that "A person can have a phone number" becomes "A person can have two phone numbers". A new field is added to a table, instead of creating a new database table for it. The result is:

- We can no longer easily create a list of all phone numbers; we'll need specific code to join 2 database columns.

- If only 1 phone number is used, the other field stays empty, wasting space (and requiring code to prevent displaying empty phone numbers).

- Any code that searches by phone number most now be duplicated to first search for `phonenumber1`, then for `phonenumber2`. Maybe the first number is for fixed phone and the second for mobile? What if someone deviates from this convention?

- We introduce a logical limitation. Suddenly, instead of 1 phone number and 1 only, we can only enter 2 phone numbers. This seems great, until we want (for instance) to add a fax number. At that point, once again we need to modify our system while we thought we were done. What if a person has 2 mobile phones and a fixed phone? What if someone has a call center with a whole range of numbers?

If instead we take the time to implement an extra table for multiple phone numbers, we'll only need to make one (albeit a bit more complex) change. We can then add as many numbers as we like, and prevent introducing logical limitations. To list all available numbers, all we do is a lookup in 1 column in the table. To distinguish what is what, maybe we'll create an additional table containing all possible types of phone number: home, office, fixed, cell, SMS, home fax, office fax and so on. Reverse lookups are also much easier.

This will also add flexibility in the future: Maybe at some point we'll be asked to add email-addresses (home, office, instant messenger...) for which we won't have to do much: Maybe we'll just add some phone number types and use regular expressions for pattern matching.

This little extra investment in time is easily won back as things are progressing, because subsequent changes will be much easier to make. Should we want a limit (3 phone numbers maximum), we can add a validation. To raise this limit, all we have to do is change a constant, instead of duplicating and altering code. Stepping back from 1-to-many to 1-to-N is simple enough, as long as you didn't cut corners before.

The following topic explains in detail how we should work to keep our data structures in shape. This will help clear up a few questions that you may still have.

3.8 Keep data structures normalized

Normalization is the practice of restructuring data structures in such a manner that they are free of duplication and free of redundancy. An added benefit of normalization is that a normalized data structure can be more easily adapted to changing requirements. The following pages show how.

There are several degrees of normalization, offering increasing levels of flexibility. The most commonly used degree of normalization is called the third normal form[9]. The third normal form defines data structures in such a way that there is a well-defined functional separation between various entities or data types.

Let us assume a table-based system. Refactoring such an existing system can be quite hard, but keeping a structure normalized can be surprisingly simple, as long as we follow a few basic principles:

1. 1-on-1 relationships can be kept in a single table.

2. 1-on-N relationships live in 2 tables, where the "N" table contains a foreign key to the "1" table.

3. N-on-N relationships should be kept in a third table, which has its own primary key. This table merely connects 2 existing tables.

---

9   At least six degrees of normalization, or normal forms, exist. The third normal form corresponds to the degree of normalization normally used in object-oriented programming.

This may seem a bit confusing at first, so let us take a look at an example. We will create a simple, one-table telephone book database. As multiple people can have the same name, we identify them by a separate key, which we will call person_id. This is not required for phone numbers, because they are their own identification. So, our simple phone book looks as follows (according to principle 1):

Table person

person_id (primary key)	person_name	phone_number
1	P. Fink	555-5782
2	M. Plow	555-3226

A new requirement just got in: Some people have more than one phone number, and we must be able to store it. As the field person_id is a primary key, it can not be duplicated in the table. We have two options: One is to add another phone number column (this is a step in the wrong direction, as discussed in previous chapters), and the other is to separate phone numbers from people. This will give us the following:

Table person

person_id (primary key)	person_name
1	P. Fink
2	M. Plow

Table phone_numbers

phone_number (primary key)	phone_number_owner (foreign key referencing person_id in table person)
555-5782	1
555-3226	2
555-3223	2

In this last table, we see how multiple phone numbers can be assigned to the same person (according to principle 2 mentioned earlier). Maybe we want to add a little free text description to each phone number; as long as it is 1 description, it can be in the same table (principle 1).

Table phone_numbers

phone_number (primary key)	phone_number_owner (foreign key)	phone_number_description
555-5782	1	home phone
555-3226	2	business
555-3223	2	home

Oops- another requirement just got in. Not only can a person have multiple phone numbers, a phone number can also be used by multiple people. So we are dealing with an N-to-N relationship here. Enter principle 3: A connector table connecting the two others together.

The structure of table `person` is unchanged. But let's add a person that will have the same phone number as M. Plow:

Table person

person_id (primary key)	person_name
1	P. Fink
2	M. Plow
3	B. Simpson

The foreign key to table `person` in table `phone_numbers` will be moved to the connector table, so it is removed from table `phone_numbers`.

Table phone_numbers

phone_number (primary key)	phone_number_ description
555-5782	home phone
555-3226	business
555-3223	home

Finally, we create the connector table and give it its own primary key. We'll have to give it a name that properly describes the information contained by the table. Because it contains phone numbers and people, perhaps this is the actual phone book. So let us simply call that table `phone_book`. It will look as follows:

Table phone_book

phonebook_ entry_id (primary key)	phone_number (foreign key referencing the primary key of table phone_numbers)	person_id (foreign key referencing the primary key of table person)
PB1	555-5782	1
PB2	555-3226	2
PB3	555-3223	2
PB4	555-3223	3

So, there we have it: Multiple people can have multiple phone numbers. But what is the point of having a primary key for each of these relationships? Well, this will allow us to store data related to combinations of a person and a phone number. For instance, we can now easily implement a call register:

Table call_register

callreg_entry (primary key)	phonebook_ entry_id (foreign key)	to_number (foreign key)	start_ time	end_ time
CR1	PB4	555-5782	12:34	01:23
CR2	PB3	555-5782	01:24	01:25
CR3	PB3	555-3226	01:26	01:27
CR4	PB4	555-5782	01:28	01:31

In conjunction with the other tables, this gives us all information about who called what number, and when.

From the previous example, it is clear when new tables should be created, and it also shows how a design might be updated to maintain flexibility. When every table contains a primary key (in a single field), this will allow us to easily find which information goes together.

When we want to keep the data structure normalized, of course some data migration may be needed once in a while. But by keeping the data structure normalized, we keep it flexible enough to adapt to almost any requirement.

In the above example, it is easy to query the structure for all phone numbers, or even for all calls to all phone numbers. The amount of duplicate code needed to interact with the structure is minimal. Should we have decided to instead add a column `phone_number_2`, not only would we have introduced a limit of 2 phone numbers per person to our system, we would also have needed to duplicate and complicate a lot of code for even the most common queries.

To finish off this topic, a few words of caution are in place. To query a structure for certain very specific information, it will be necessary to join the data of a lot of tables together. If this is done carelessly, your query may hit almost the entire database. This can cause performance to drop immensely. Read the chapter "**Keep the Cartesian product small**" (page 290) for a possible way to remedy this situation.

It would seem that implementing every relationship as N-to-N would solve all problems. Be careful: you will then be well on your way of designing your own DBMS, which is usually counter-productive and comes with the risk of over-analyzing.

3.9 Beware of over-analyzing

As important as it is to perform a thorough analysis of the system that we're building, it is possible to take things a step too far. A proper information analysis allows our client a great deal of flexibility, but we cannot escape building systems with some limitations. The risk of over-analyzing is to get stuck in analysis, never getting anything done. This is a common anti-pattern known as *analysis paralysis*.

But how do we recognize where to stop analyzing? For best productivity, in most cases, you'll want to stop analyzing at the point where you start designing a design tool. At that point, you are no longer designing what the client asked but something different altogether. The end user doesn't need to have ultimate power to design their own system. They expect you to do this for them. It may still be possible to justify designing such a tool in company time, between projects.

By the time you've started designing a design tool *in itself*, you've probably already gone a step too far for most practical purposes, into the deepest realms of information theory. This can be a wonderful trip in which a great deal can be learned, but you should probably limit these trips to your own time.

Chapter 4

Guarantee preconditions

If all error-causing conditions are prevented, no errors will occur. This seemingly trivial statement is the cornerstone of writing bug-free code. There are many ways to improve on code and user interfaces, which can be traced back to this first statement. The following pages of this chapter are a selection of these techniques. When followed closely, these techniques will help you write robust code time after time, rather than leaving the quality of your code to chance.

4.1 Perform initialization

Before any variable is used, it needs to be initialized to a sensible value. In some cases our programming language does this for us, but in other languages the result of the following piece of code can not be guaranteed, as declaring variables does not equals initialization:

```
int x()
{
    int a; // uninitialized!
    int b; // uninitialized!
    int c; // initialized in next line
    c=a+b;
    return c; // can be anything
}
```

Initializing variables with a default value prevents unpredictable behaviour. When porting code from one language to another, this will greatly influence the reliability of the ported code.

In object-oriented programming, initializing all properties of an object class is even more important. When object properties remain uninitialized by the constructor, this can cause the program to crash, but this will only happen when the destructor of the object is called. This makes it extra difficult to find the cause of the error.

4.2 Verify preconditions

Although at first sight the following code looks fine, further inspection will reveal some mistakes.

```
int a(object object1)
{
    int x=object1.getobject2().getvalue();
    return x;
}
```

The mistakes are not syntactic but semantic in nature. The code is semantically wrong, because:

- When object1==null, the program will crash.

- When getobject2() returns the value null, the program will crash.

If we're lucky, the problem will never reveal itself in runtime, but we should not depend on luck for our code to work.

The cause of the problem is that variable object1 is being used without verifying its value, which allows the code to be called with values that crash it. Likewise, the return value of function getobject2() is being used without verifying its value.

In the following code, this problem is solved by checking all variables before use:

```
int a(object object1)
{
    int x;
    if (object1!=null)
    {
        object object2;
        object2=object1.getobject2();
        if (object2!=null)
        {
            x=object2.getvalue();
        }
        else
        {
            throw new exception("AARGH!!");
        }
    }
    else
    {
        throw new exception("OUCH!!");
    }
    return x;
}
```

By checking all variables before their first use, and all return values of functions as well, we can properly throw exceptions and handle errors depending on what went wrong, rather than letting the program crash hard and not having a clue. In some cases, throwing exceptions may not even be necessary; just because an object has an undefined value, this doesn't always mean we're dealing with an invalid condition. We'll just have to consciously distinguish between these situations.

Some people will prefer the following variation of the above code. By inverting the IF expressions, the ELSE branches could be eliminated. This will show more clearly which condition triggers each exception.

```
int a(object object1)
{
    int x;

    if (object1==null)
    {
        throw new exception("OUCH!!");
    }
    object object2=object1.getobject2();
    if (object2==null)
    {
        throw new exception("AARGH!!");
    }

    /* All preconditions are OK,
       no further tests needed. */
    x=object2.getvalue();
    return x;
}
```

Functionally, both pieces of code are exactly identical.

The main conclusions for this topic are:

- Failing to check preconditions is the main cause of uncontrolled crashes.

- By splitting up your statements, rather than trying to write everything on a single line, exceptions can be prevented.

4.3 Decide on precondition responsibility

There are two opposing philosophies when it comes to precondition checks. One is that subroutines should be responsible for checking their input; the other is that they never should be called with incorrect values. As is often the case, there is no absolute truth, as will be shown by the following.

Imagine a subroutine that draws a pixel on the screen. There are two possible scenarios: either the subroutine itself checks its input parameters, or the caller has to make sure that it never calls the subroutine with incorrect parameters. In the first scenario, the subroutine might be implemented as follows:

```
function drawpixel(x,y,color)
{
    if (x<0)                 { return; }
    if (x>=SCREEN_WIDTH)     { return; }
    if (y<0)                 { return; }
    if (y>=SCREEN_HEIGHT)    { return; }
    if (color<0)             { return; }
    if (color>255)           { return; }
    writemem(y*SCREEN_WIDTH+x,color);
}
```

If we call the subroutine with coordinates that are outside the boundaries of the screen, it will simply not draw anything. The behaviour of the subroutine is defined for every possible input parameter. As a result, the subroutine will be very reliable. Nothing will crash it or cause it to show unexpected behaviour.

Now imagine we call this subroutine from another subroutine: one that draws straight lines. To better serve its users, this line drawing routine allows specifying coordinates outside the screen boundaries. Rather than calculating where a line intersects the screen, it simply calls the pixel-drawing routine with any coordinates that come up. This doesn't crash the pixel-drawing function; in fact, it shows lines perfectly clipped at the screen boundaries, intersecting the screen at exactly the right positions.

As a result, the line-drawing function can stay as simple as possible.

Unfortunately, there are a few drawbacks to that approach. First of all, the line drawing function will make a lot of unnecessary function calls when the endpoints of the line fall outside the screen boundaries. But even when the line drawing function makes sure to clip the line in such a way that it will only draw pixels within the screen boundaries, CPU cycles are wasted. If both of the endpoints of the line are within the screen boundaries, why does the pixel-drawing function need to verify all the pixels in between?

The screen handling of the original PC-XT BIOS was designed in a similar manner: All BIOS functions checked their own values. The BIOS would never crash, but screen handling was notoriously slow.

The second philosophy assigns responsibility of the correctness of the function parameters to the caller, rather than the subroutine being called. As a result, the functions being called could be much lighter and simpler.

When a function is only called with correct parameters, there is no point for that function in checking all its input parameters.

A pixel-drawing subroutine might then be as simple as:

```
function drawpixel(x,y,color)
{
    writemem(y*SCREEN_WIDTH+x,color);
}
```

This code is lightning fast compared to the code with all the internal checks, but it is not quite as reliable. Of course, in this case we assume that the correctness of the function is the responsibility of the caller. In our test code, we make sure to verify the correctness of the caller by adding assertions to our code, which will abort the code as soon as a caller breaks the rules:

```
function drawpixel(x,y,color)
{
    assert ((x>=0) && (x<SCREEN_WIDTH));
    assert ((y>=0) && (y<SCREEN_HEIGHT));
    assert ((color>=0) && (color<=255));
    writemem(y*SCREEN_WIDTH+x,color);
}
```

This 'asserted' code will be automatically removed in the production version, effectively leaving the above code without checks. However, if somehow some untested combination of conditions causes the subroutine to be called with incorrect parameters, this will result in pixels being drawn at the wrong position, in the best case scenario. If we are not so lucky, it may cause all kinds of deliciously unpredictable behaviour such as corrupting data, crashing the computer, or compromising security.

Which philosophy you follow depends on the requirements. If the pixel-drawing code would run on an arcade game machine, speed might be crucial. If it would run on the on-board software of an airplane, reliability might be more important.

Alternatively, we may choose a combination of both philosophies, and get the best of both worlds:

```
function drawpixel_raw(x,y,color)
{
    writemem(y*screenwidth+x,color);
}


function drawpixel(x,y,color)
{
    if (x<0)                 { return; }
    if (x>=SCREEN_WIDTH)     { return; }
    if (y<0)                 { return; }
    if (y>=SCREEN_HEIGHT)    { return; }
    if (color<0)             { return; }
    if (color>255)           { return; }
    drawpixel_raw(x,y,color);
}

function drawline(x1,y1,x2,y2,color)
{
    // Check preconditions, clip as needed.
    // Then use drawpixel_raw for speed.
}
```

Especially in object-oriented environments this may be a sensible approach; In that case, the 'raw' version would likely be made private for safety reasons.

The main conclusions of this topic are:

- For best reliability, code should be responsible for checking its own preconditions. However, this causes a performance loss.

- For best performance, if we are careful never to call subroutines with incorrect arguments, we can leave out these checks, at the risk of introducing unpredictable behaviour.

4.4 Be aware of invalidated preconditions

In the previous paragraph, we have seen that for best reliability each piece of code needs to be responsible for its own preconditions. Normally, we think of preconditions and postconditions as existing only at the beginning and end of subroutines. In reality, the point of return of a function call, too, needs to have its preconditions guaranteed.

Any time when a variable changes, its precondition checks may be invalidated.

The importance of re-validating a variable after it changes, is quite obvious when it is the result of a function that returns an object or a pointer. The following, although syntactically sound, is semantically wrong:

```
Object myobject=GetObject(objID);
myobject.do_something();
```

The problem with the above is that the function can return a `null` object, which will cause the program to crash as soon as a method of `myobject` is called. The code on the following page fixes this:

```
/*  object myobject has been checked,
    everything is safe and sound
*/

myobject=GetObject(objID);
/*
    function call completed- we must now
    check the post-call preconditions
    for all influcenced variables, for the
    rest of code.

    The call to GetObject influences
    myobject, so that is what we must check.
*/

if (myobject==null)
{
    /* precondition check
       for remaining code */
    throw new Exception("Whoops...");
}
/* Everything is safe and sound again */
myobject.do_something();
```

In some cases, the result of the function call is still processed further before it is used and passed on to another function call. If that function checks its own preconditions, we should not need to do it as well- but we might perform the check anyway to be on the safe side.

In some cases, the return value of a function is part of a larger plan. For instance, in a web page generator, the result may be a single HTML element, and the return values of many function calls are put together to form a single piece of output. In such situations, there seems to be little added value in checking the results, but some checks (such as verifying maximum string length of the resulting page) of course still have their use.

Chapter 5

Mimimize complexity

The main strategy we have in keeping software systems maintainable, is to keep their complexity to a minimum. To be able to do this, first we must understand the factors that make a system complex:

- The number of different states a program can be in

- The degree in which code depends on other code (requiring us to read more code before we can perform maintenance tasks)

- Inconsistency or chaos

The following paragraphs will hand you a few techniques that will help reduce complexity by avoiding the above causes.

5.1 Write less code

Often code written by master programmers is deceivingly simple; to solve a problem, master programmers will typically need to write fewer lines of code than novice programmers. Code written by master programmers will typically contain smaller functions, and each function typically uses fewer variables.

The fewer variables our code contains, the fewer states our code can be in. Smaller, less stateful functions will be easier to test and debug than big ones.

Writing less code does not mean 'cramming as many operations as possible in a single line'. Instead, we want our code to contain fewer *atomic* instructions. The fewer *atomic* instructions the code contains, the less complex it will be. What I mean by *atomic* instructions are instructions that can not be split up in several smaller instructions, in the language they are written in. For instance, the instruction

```
a[b++]=1;
```

is not atomic, because it can be split up. We can rewrite it as the following, which can not be split up any further:

```
a[b]=1;
b++;
```

If you are coding and there is a little voice in the back of your head saying "There must be a simpler, shorter way to code this", there probably is. Take a step back from your code and try to find it. If you don't see it, maybe a co-worker will. Consult them in case of doubt.

5.2 Avoid global variables

Global variables are variables that can be accessed from anywhere in your program. To the novice, this may seem like a wonderfully practical idea, but in reality using global variables is one of the worst programming practices there is.

Global variables are an especially big problem in event-driven code, because any event can alter their value. As such their value cannot be guaranteed without verifying the entire system. Most systems nowadays are event-driven, so this is a big deal. Event-driven code that uses global variables is only predictable when the contents of the variable are verified every single time that the variable is used, except when the variable is protected from changes by some locking mechanism.

Another problem with global variables is that they will make the code less transparent, because the same input parameters for a function may give a different result from one time to another.

```
int a(int b)
{
    global c;
    if (c==10)
    {
        /* by now, newly checked global c
           may already have been changed
           by an event- result of a() is
           unpredictable
        */
        b=c+c;
    }
    return b;
}
```

In this example, the global variable c is declared for illustrational purposes only. In most programming languages, globals can be used without being declared.

There are a number of problems with the above source. First of all, it is theoretically possible (in case of event driven code) that the value of the global variable has changed between the moment that the precondition check was performed and the moment that the variable was used for the calculation. This renders the return value of the code unpredictable, and therefore makes the function unreliable.

In addition, the interface definition of the code doesn't reveal that the code uses a global variable. It is not enough to read the function header to fully understand what parts of the system influence it, and what parts are influenced by it; to fully understand the scope of the function, one must read the function in its entirety- and hope it doesn't call other functions which exhibit the same problem. If functions use global variables carelessly, this may cause a snowball effect, as it could mean programmers need to fully understand the system *in its entirety* before they can safely start working on it without risking to break existing code. Because of this, systems that contain a lot of global variables will typically require much more time to get accustomed to than systems without globals.

The following piece of code solves these problems. The value of local variable c can not be influenced by external factors. In addition, the function prototype shows fellow programmers that the outcome of the function is influenced by more than just a single input value.

```
int a(session sessionobject,int b)
{
    int c; /* local variable is safe from
                manipulation by external
                events */
    if (sessionobject==null)
    {
        throw new exception("AAIEEE!");
    }
    c=sessionobject.c;
    if (c==10)
    {
        b=c+c;
    }
    return b;
}
```

In this example it is assumed a session object exists which may hold many (formerly) global variables. In this case, only property c of the session object is used.

One might argue that it would be better to pass just variable sessionobject.c to the function, instead of the session object. Depending on the context of the problem, this may be true. It will make even more clear what exactly it is that is used or influenced by the function. The trade-off is that the interface of the function might need to change more often, breaking compatibility between different versions of the function.

Ideally, our interface definition would make it clear if the function can or cannot alter the session object. In this case, the session object is only read, not written. Some languages allow specifying whether a variable is intended for input or output, which will help inform fellow programmers what to expect from the function:

```
int a(in session sessionobject,in int b);
```

This shows that when calling function `a`, we won't have to worry about changes in the session object. Languages in the C/C++ family define similar behaviour with the `const` keyword, to indicate that a variable should never be modified by the called function. It is considered good practice to default to using this keyword for all input-only variables.

Many of the objections of using global *variables* do not apply to global *constants*. Because their value never changes, a single precondition check is sufficient to guarantee that their value fulfills all requirements. Also, if their value is wrong, we will know where to look for that wrong value.

Even so, the use of globals (either constants or variables) typically indicates a lack of modularity. Functions or procedures that use globals are usually hard to re-use in other systems, because they depend too much on the environment of the system for which they were written.

That said, there are a very small number of exceptional situations in which the use of global variables is somewhat acceptable.

A rare situation where using global variables is acceptable, is for memoization (function result caching), in case the language lacks static variables. Any global variable should then be set and used by *one and only one* function. This greatly reduces their problematic behaviour, because the global variables are used in a manner that mimics local variables.

In such a case, it is recommendable to keep the global variable definition near the function that uses it, and to add a comment indicating that it should be accessed by that function only. The function, along with its globally declared result, can then still be easily reused in other code. See the chapter on memoization (page 203) for more details on this.

Even to store configuration information, it may already be better not to use global variables but a configuration- or session object. The configuration of a program is generally read from file or database only once, and as such the globals in fact act mostly as constants. However, using global variables in this context already impacts code reusability. Using a configuration- or session object reduces this impact by channelling all configuration information through function parameters.

Finally, keep in mind that carelessly used member variables in classes can exhibit some of the problematic behaviour as global variables, albeit in a smaller scope. Like is the case with global variables, most of this problematic behaviour instantly disappears when the value of the member variable is set in one place only. Setting member variables as private will protect them from external changes and will improve the modularity of your system.

5.3 Keep minimal scope and extent

The fewer variables are used in a piece of code, the fewer different states the code can be in. The complexity of the code is reduced, which is a Good Thing (as we will see in chapter **Write Unit Tests**, see page 267). This not only suggests we should prefer local scope over using global variables, but also to keep the lifetime (or extent) of local variables as small as possible.

We could count the number of lines of code in which a variable is effectively in use, to get an idea of the complexity of the code. The lower the resulting number, the less complex the code. Take a look at the following code.

```
int x=1;   // first line where x is used
int y=2;   // first line where y is used
write(x);  // last line where x is used
write(y);  // last line where y is used
```

The effects of variables x and y in this snippet span 3 lines each from where they are first used to where they are last used. This potentially increases the complexity of the code, and makes it harder to read. Alternatively, we could write the code as:

```
int x=1;   // first line where x is used
write(x);  // last line where x is used
int y=2;   // first line where y is used
write(y);  // last line where y is used
```

In this case, each variable only spans 2 lines from their first to their last use. Also, there is no overlap in their usage. As a result, the average number of states that each line can have is reduced. Of course, in this small example the benefit is minimal.

Some languages allow defining block scope; in such a case, contrary to the first snippet, the latter code allows itself to be rewritten as:

```
{
    int a=1;
    write(a);
}
{
    int b=2;
    write(b);
}
```

In the last case, the two snippets are completely separated from one another, meaning the compiler helps us guarantee that one snippet of code can never influence the results of the other. This helps us further minimize the statefulness of each line of code. Also, the fact that the two snippets of code *can* be completely separated from one another proves better modularity over the initial example.

Small scope and extent help keep the number of states of code to a minimum, making the code less complex and more modular. This in turn makes it easier to rewrite our code into functions (a benefit even more clear if each snippet contains more lines). Because of this, even in languages that do not support block scope, it is useful to keep minimal scope and extent.

5.4 Prevent side effects by functions

For a function to be as useful as possible, there must be no doubt about what it does, preferably without the need to consult a manual or to read the entire code of the function. To this end, it is necessary that function is deterministic; that is, given the same input, a function always returns the same result. Whenever a function affects the state of the system other than by its own return value, the function is said to have a side effect, or to be *unorthogonal*.

Changing global variables from a function is a particularly bad side effect. It may not have much impact on the function itself, but it can make other functions unpredictable. If several functions all set a global variable to a certain value, and one of them is incorrect, how will you find the wrong function among the suspects?

By making functions deterministic and stateless, they will be easier to test automatically by means of unit tests (see page 267). Indeterministic functions may grow so many different possible states that automated testing will be impossible.

State implies a memory effect. As such, less state implies a more scalable, less complex system. This is wonderfully demonstrated by the world wide web, which was originally designed as a stateless system. Given enough bandwidth, a completely stateless web site can serve billions of users with near-zero memory requirements.

5.5 Pull vs. push methodology

In the previous paragraph we talked about side effects of functions. The same principle applies in a wider context as well. We most commonly see this in user interfaces that act as database front end.

For simplicity, we can see this in an object-oriented context. Consider a field object. A field is a data structure which has a data type and a value, and a piece of code (a method) associated to it that performs a calculation.

We speak of pull methodology when a field object exclusively calculates its own value: it reads values from other fields, performs a calculation and comes to a result. It is as if the field object 'pulls' the data towards itself. Given the same set of source data, the result is always predictable. Recalculating the field has no side effects in the rest of the system. Note that the field only reads information from other fields, but it does not write to them, so it can never leave the rest of the system in a corrupt state.

In push methodology, a field may take the initiative to update one or more other fields- to 'push' data to them, as it were. For instance, field A, B, C and D may all write to field E. If any of the code in field A, B, C or D is wrong, this will result in an incorrect value for field E. It will be difficult to debug the system, because a wrong value in field E can have so many different causes. In a situation like this, field E behaves very much like a global variable.

To create the most consistent, maintenance free system possible, don't let fields tell other fields what their value is. Let every field calculate its own value. Allow any field to read the value of other fields, but do not allow them to write another value to them.

There is a link between the concept of using pull- vs. push methodology and information analysis. In case of pull-methodology, the value of a variable is only calculated in *one* place, which makes it easier to maintain the value of that variable correct. In case of push-methodology, the value of a variable may be calculated in *many* places. As a result, when we encounter a bug, we need to visit all of these many places to find out where things went wrong.

Chapters **Use information analysis in UI design** (page 167) and **Write knowledge-free functions** (page 244) help to explain this further.

5.6 Small projects instead of big ones

In my experience, the most effective way to guarantee that a project will fail, is to attempt to build a system that does everything: contact management, managing business processes, stock control, invoicing, reporting, and so on. This applies to custom-built software as much as it does to mass-produced software. At some point, unless things are extremely well-managed, systems will get so complex that they collapse under their own weight.

At the same time, the same complexity will cause a big duplication of functionality. We can easily observe this: How many user-lists are there present within your company? Probably you have a windows login, an email account, bug tracking account, time sheet software account, an entry in salary administration, a human resource record, and so on, and so forth.

World wide, your name may be subscribed into hundreds of user lists, and chances are, probably you've built a login box or user administration module several times. Why is it that after decades and decades of business automation, we're still building modules for such trivial tasks?

If we are to build a simple, one-form system such as a user database, there is a big probability that the project will succeed. Chances that the information in there can be exported to other systems are pretty good too, provided that the data is properly structured.

In a business environment, if we build several small systems instead of one huge monolithic system, not only will we increase the chance for the project to be successful, we enhance reusability of each small module and possibly make the business itself more efficient: it is obvious that entering employee data only once will cost less time than doing the same ten times. It will also help guarantee consistency of the data within the cooperation.

A key factor in the success of this approach is that we have a way to transparently synchronize data from one system to another. We can either write our own code to synchronize the data, or use one of the several commercial solutions that exist for this purpose.

5.7 Avoid GOTO

You probably already know to avoid `goto` statements, and thanks to Edsger Dijkstra[10], we have practically abolished the use of this statement from our programming languages. As such, telling you to avoid `goto` statements is probably a cliché, but this text would not be complete without a few words on the subject.

As it turns out, most languages still contain the `goto` statement. Also, the code that our compilers generate is full of jump instructions, both conditional and unconditional. So why aren't jumps or `goto` statements a problem in compiled code?

The answer is *structure*. The jump statements themselves are not the problem. In fact our code would not work without them. The problem is *how* we use these statements. The following are the key reasons to avoid using `goto` statements:

- Jumping between functions (should your compiler allow it) may mess up the call stack which is normally managed by the compiler;

- Jumping to any location in code will invalidate all precondition checks preceding that location. This is also why we should consider all preconditions invalid at the returning point of any function;

10 Go To Statement Considered Harmful, by Edsger W. Dijkstra, Letter to Communications of the ACM (CASM) Vol. 11 no. 3, March 1968, pp. 147-148. Online at http://www.acm.org/classics/oct95.

- When jumping between different scopes, the concept of scope breaks down. Suddenly everything should be treated as global scope, which implies extra complexity;

- Without a mechanism to enforce program structure, using goto statements likely results in "spaghetti code" which is not reusable and almost impossible to maintain.

- These reasons aside, your programming language most likely provides you with better, more structured alternatives.

This last point gives some room for discussion. What if your programming language is of such limited syntax that it does not provide you with the alternative that you need?

The answer is, when the syntax of the language we work with is limited, this should not limit us from expressing logic. The long obsolete Sinclair ZX81 computer had a BASIC dialect which did not support ELSE as part of an IF statement. It was impossible to write the following:

```
10 IF A>B THEN MAX=A ELSE MAX=B
20 REM REST OF PROGRAM
```

Instead, to obtain the exact same effect, a programmer had to write:

```
10 IF A>B THEN GOTO 40
20 LET MAX=B
30 GOTO 50
40 LET MAX=A
50 REM REST OF PROGRAM
```

The second program uses a `goto` statement, the first does not.

Of course this doesn't make the first program any better than the second one. As the programmer of the second piece of code really had no choice but to use `goto`, this merely shows that the programming *language* in which the first piece of code was written, was better suited for the purpose. The program itself is equally good.

Although the code contains the `goto` statement, there is no 'spaghetti code' going on. Both pieces of code share the following elegant program structure:

is A greater than B?	
YES	NO
MAX=A	MAX=B
(Rest of program)	

Syntax aside, the semantics of the former two snippets of code are exactly identical. This shows us that structure and syntax are independent of each other. It also implies that to write reusable, modular code, structure plays a more important role than syntax. The underlying reason for the discussion about the `goto` statement has always been the structure of the written code, rather than the syntax used to obtain that structure.

Although the improved syntax of modern programming languages is a big help to writing structured programs, it does not guarantee it. As such, no matter what syntax you use, you should never use it as an excuse for writing poorly structured code.

In an effort to avoid `goto` statements at all costs (or perhaps as an excuse for writing unstructured code) some programmers choose to implement state machines. By embedding a `case` statement inside a loop, we can cause ourselves all the structural problems of `goto` statements *and* negatively impact program performance[11]:

```
PROG_END=9999;
line=0;
while (line<PROG_END)
{
    line+=10;
    switch (line)
    {
        case 10:
            if (a>b) line=40 /* goto */;
            break;
        case 20:
            max=b; break;
        case 30:
            line=50 /* goto */;  break;
        case 40:
            max=a; break;
        case 50:
            /* REST OF PROGRAM */
            line=PROG_END; break;
    }
}
```

Such code would be better off being rewritten *with* `goto` statements: it would perform better and have a much simpler structure. It would still need rewriting, but it would be easier to rewrite into proper code than the state machine version.

---

11 Attentive readers will recognize that this code is equivalent to the previous two code snippets.

Chapter 6

Improve your code

In the previous chapter we briefly discussed how program structure can help in writing maintainable code. Regardless of the language you work in, you will have used decision branches (if, elseif, else), loops (while, for, do, repeat), selections (switch, case) and of course sub-programs or functions.

This chapter will dig a bit deeper than usual into these basic constructs, to help you write code with the cleanest possible structure. This will result in code that is easier to read, more memory efficient, faster, more modular, easier to debug and even easier to prove correct.

6.1 Program Structure Diagrams

Before we dive into the actual material, let us first take a look at how we will be graphically representing program flow.

Traditional flowcharts have long had their time. Although being a useful tool to draw program flow, they made it too easy to draw unstructured programs. Things got a bit better when structured programming languages such as Pascal took the place of less structured programming languages such as FORTRAN. In the spirit of structured programming, flow charts also became more structured, and made way for Nassi-Schneidermann diagrams (also known as Program Structure Diagrams[12]).

Unfortunately, even when we use structured programming languages and PSDs, we can still create unstructured code, as will be shown briefly.

To present the structure of a piece of code graphically, we will represent program structure in the following manner:

---

12 Program Structure Diagrams help people to think of their code as blocks that are executed front to back, a block at a time. Traditionally, diagonal lines are used for IF statements. For simplicity, in this text, we abandon the diagonal lines. This allows us to represent these diagrams in any environment that can handle tables.

- IF statements:

expression	
true	**false**
code to be executed when expression is true	code to be executed when expression is false

- SWITCH/CASE statements:

expression		
value1	**value2**	**value3**
code to be executed when expression equals value1	code to be executed when expression equals value2	code to be executed when expression equals value3

- WHILE/FOR loops:

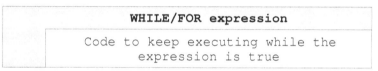

WHILE/FOR expression
Code to keep executing while the expression is true

- DO..WHILE (or REPEAT..UNTIL) loops:

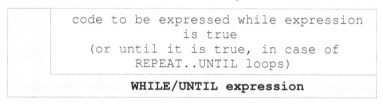

code to be expressed while expression is true (or until it is true, in case of REPEAT..UNTIL loops)
WHILE/UNTIL expression

For best program structure, in general, we will be wanting to draw Program Structure Diagrams that as clearly as possible show all the possible code paths and their respective results.

The following shows us an unstructured PSD:

statement			
if			
true	**false**		
statement	**if**		
	true	**false**	
	statement	statement	
	if		
	true	**false**	
	statement	statement	

The problem with the above diagram is that it does not clearly show all possible ways the code can be executed, because some code paths re-join after branching. As a result, if we want to write a unit test for our code, we will have some trouble to make sure all paths are covered.

In this text, we will pursue code that is structured in such a way that each code path stands by itself, and can be traced back to the unique set of conditions that led to that code path. This is done by making sure that of each if statement, one branch always extends to the end of the code block.

To allow tracing back the code path to the unique set of conditions causing it, once code paths are separated, they will not join again. The one exception to this rule is joining the code paths by a single termination clause, as shown on page 133 and beyond. This will help us to debug our program and to prevent resource leaks.

The following diagram is structured in such a manner that all code paths can be traced back to their cause:

statement			
if			
true	false		
	if		
	true	false	
		if	
		true	false
statement	statement	statement	statement

Note the diagonal structure of the if statements. By following this structure, in an instant we can see how many possible code paths there are by simply counting the amount of columns at the bottom of the diagram.

As it turns out, keeping such a structure is a pretty good indicator when to split up a function. Whenever the structure can no longer be maintained, it is usually a good idea to create a new function.

When you write code according to the above structure, you will find there is little need to ever draw diagrams of your code to make crystal clear what it does. When your code returns a value, structuring it as above will allow you to make sure that all possible code paths have a defined result, which in turn will make your code more robust.

Now that we have this settled, let us continue exploring the ways in which we may improve our code.

6.2 Keep logically related code together

In some cases, programmers write ELSE in an IF statement that ends a method or function, for example:

```
if (somethingIsWrong)
{
    throw new Exception("Something is wrong");
}
else
{
    block_b();
}
block_c();
```

Using an ELSE statement here unnecessarily increases the amount of indentation of the code, which leaves us with less horizontal space per line of code.

Also, it may confuse us into thinking that statements block_b(); and block_c(); do not logically belong together, whereas the PSD shows us that in reality they do:

if (somethingIsWrong)	
true	**false**
throw new Exception ("Something is wrong");	block_b();
	block_c();

By throwing an exception, the procedure is terminated, whereas
`block_b()` and `block_c()` are always executed under the same
conditions. Because of this, it is better to write:

```
if (somethingIsWrong)
{
    throw new Exception("Something is wrong");
}
block_b();
block_c();
```

6.3 Split up compound IF expressions

Code may break when we do not work atomically, because
preconditions are overlooked. This was already demonstrated in
an earlier example in this text:

```
int a(object object1)
{
    int x=object1.getobject2().getvalue();
    return x;
}
```

What happens when `getobject2()` returns the value `null`? The
code breaks, the program crashes. Less obvious is that the same
problem might occur in compound conditions in IF statements:

```
if ((object1!=null)
    && (object1.getobject2()!=null))
{
    /* do something */
}
```

The above IF statement will only work correctly when only part
of the expression is evaluated, and if we can guarantee that the
expression is evaluated from the left to the right. If this is how
our compiler or interpreter works[13], there is no real problem, but
why submit ourselves to possible quirks of the language in
which we have written the program?

We can guarantee that things always work as we intended by
splitting up the compound IF statement into two atomic IF
statements, as is shown next:

---

13 Often it is, as many programming languages default to lazy evaluation.

```
if (object1!=null)
{
    if (object1.getobject2()!=null)
    {
        /* do something */
    } // else? (1)
}
```

There are several benefits of this method:

- We don't *assume* that the code breaks out of the `if` statement when `(object1==null)`, we *guarantee* it. Even if our compiler does not perform 'lazy evaluation' optimizing, no more is evaluated than necessary and our program won't crash.

- We motivate ourselves to think of all possible combinations of conditions. The original statement never made us think about `(1)`, what to do when `(object1! =null)` and `(object1.getobject2==null)`.

- By splitting the conditions, we can generate more specific error messages:

```
if (object1==null)
{
    throw new exception("OOMPH!");
}

if (object1.getobject2()==null)
{
    throw new exception("GASP!");
}
/* do something */
```

Because only one condition is evaluated at a time, the code is also easier to inspect in runtime. Not only will single-step debugging be easier, debugging by means of a log file will be as well.

The concept of splitting up compound expressions into atomic ones inside IF statements has similar benefits when applied to the logical OR. The following example shows this.

```
if ((age<MINIMUM_AGE) || (age>MAXIMUM_AGE))
{
    throw new exception(
        "Age not within range!");
}
```

By rewriting the compound expression in this manner, we will be able to more precisely define the error that has occurred:

```
if (age<MINIMUM_AGE)
{
    throw new exception(
      "Person is too young!");
}

if (age>MAXIMUM_AGE)
{
    throw new exception(
      "Person is too old!");
}
```

Rather than nesting one IF statement inside another IF statement, a logical OR can be expressed by following one IF statement by another (when each exits the function) or by using an ELSE IF construction.

Finally, there is yet another type of logical OR misfit that we sometimes run into. It goes something like this:

```
if ((age>=MINIMUM_AGE)||(license==true))
{
    do_something_useful();
    if (age>=MINIMUM_AGE)
    {
        // old enough
        do_something_specific();
    }
    if (license==true)
    {
        // too young but has a license
        do_something_else();
    }
}
```

Although structurally sound, the compound expression in the outer if statement makes it necessary to repeat the individual parts of this expression in the inner if statements, causing an unnecessary performance impact.

From a readability perspective, there are four possible code paths, but the path where both expressions are true is not explicitly represented in the code. Should we wish to log a message when both expressions are true, we will have to write an additional IF statement to deal with that situation, which will increase the performance overhead even further:

```
if ((license==true)&&(age>=MINIMUM_AGE))
{
    log("both situations are true");
}
```

To resolve these problems, we can first write out all possibilities that the above code can represent, then use this to write simpler code. By reading the code, we will find that these are all possible conditions and outcomes for the code above:

age >= minimum	license == true	do something useful	do something specific	do something else
FALSE	FALSE	No	No	No
FALSE	TRUE	Yes	No	Yes
TRUE	FALSE	Yes	Yes	No
TRUE	TRUE	Yes	Yes	Yes

The benefit of writing out all these possibilities is that we will be able to guarantee that no combinations are ever forgotten, which will come in handy when we want to create unit tests that cover all possible code paths. Of course there is a limitation to what is practical. If we have thousands of combinations, we may need to rethink our strategy.

By using the table above to rewrite the IF statement one sub-expression at a time, we come to the following result which clearly represents all code paths:

```
if (age>=MINIMUM_AGE)
{
    // code path A
    do_something_useful();
    do_something_specific();
    if (license==true)
    {
        // code path 1
        do_something_else();
    }
    // else { // code path 2 }
}
else
{
    // code path B
    if (license==true)
    {
        // code path 3
        do_something_useful();
        do_something_else();
    }
    // else { // code path 4 }
}
```

In the rewritten code, every expression is only evaluated once, and only if needed, so the code will perform better. Also, all required comparisons are already present: If we want to log each possible code path, this does not require adding extra `if` statements to the code.

The added comments also show that the code better represents every possible code path, both before and after the code paths split.

By rewriting the code in this manner, the extent of each expression is reduced. This makes the code more readable and easier to abstract into functions, should we wish to do so.

Additionally, by having written out all combinations of expressions and their results, we will have paved the way for creating a data driven version of our function. This may be useful if we want to give more power to our users while cutting down on the maintenance of our system.

6.4 Reduce duplication in IF statements

Each IF statement can have two branches: the THEN branch and the ELSE branch. The THEN branch is the branch that is executed when the expression defined for the IF statements is logically true, whereas the ELSE branch is the branch that is executed otherwise.

To prevent redundant code and the added maintenance associated with it, it is recommendable to keep the content of each branch as brief as possible. The following counter-example shows the common situation where this was not yet done.

```
if (a==1)
{
    initialize();
    do_something();
    finalize();
}
else
{
    initialize();
    do_something();
    do_something_else();
    finalize();
}
```

There is a good chance that both branches need to be updated in a quite similar manner as the code is being developed further and further. As this happens, it becomes less and less obvious that the different branches are actually quite similar and that the updates need to be made to both branches, increasing the probability that bugs are introduced in the code.

In the example above, certain lines of code are equal in both branches, so these operations will be executed regardless of what the expression evaluates to. In other words, it makes no sense to duplicate them into both the THEN or ELSE branches; as these statements are basically executed unconditionally, there is in fact no need to have them inside the IF statement at all.

The code below yields exactly the same result as the code above, but the redundancy issue has been resolved. The result is reduced maintenance, and the code has become more compact, allowing us to see a bigger part of the logical flow on the same screen surface.

```
initialize();
do_something();
if (a==1)
{
    // empty THEN branch
}
else
{
    do_something_else();
}
finalize();
```

We should get rid of the empty THEN branch. We do this by inverting the IF expression and switching around the THEN and ELSE branches. We can then remove the empty ELSE branch.

The final refactored code will then look as follows:

```
initialize();
do_something();
if (a!=1)
{
    do_something_else();
}
finalize();
```

This shows us more clearly which part of the code is subject to conditional execution.

6.5 Use atomic statements

Especially Perl and C programmers like to cram a lot of operations in a single line of code. This is bad form; it makes code more sensitive to errors and more troublesome to debug.

Consider the following line of C code:

```
a[++i]=b[++j];
```

Obviously, some element from array `b` is copied to array `a`, but what about the indices? Which of the two is incremented first? Also, due to the way the statements are written down, the bounds of the arrays are not checked. As a result, the programmer must check if the indices are one *below* the maximum. For clarity, it would be better to write the above code as follows:

```
++i;
// bounds checking for a[i] goes here
++j;
// bounds checking for b[j] goes here
a[i]=b[j];
```

This notation disambiguates the order in which the atomic instructions are executed and allows for bounds checking, while still allowing the compiler to take advantage of processor-specific optimizations (i.e. translating the ++ operator to an increment instruction). As is the case with splitting up IF statements into their atomic counterparts, this will also facilitate debugging.

Another example is calling functions in `if` statements. This is especially troublesome when done in compound `if` statements (as outlined in **Split up compound IF expressions**, page 112).

The following example shows possible problems with this.

```
if (employee.getcompany()!=null)
{
    write('Company name is:');
    write(employee.getcompany().name);
}
```

As we see, one problem is that by performing the function call in the `if` statement, we will need to perform the call again later on. This is not always the case, of course, but chances that we will be wasting processing power are increased.

There is no guarantee that the code will return the same result every time. Some time will elapse between the two function calls. If the given employee is fired between function calls, the system will crash. In other words, the code is not suitable for use in a multi-tasking system unless made thread-safe by some kind of locking mechanism.

Third, depending on your debugging style and tools, debugging will be more difficult when dealing with function results rather than with variables, because it is hard to find a place in code which allows us to inspect the state of the system. The following code solves all of these problems, just by splitting up compound statements into atomic ones:

```
object company=employee.getcompany();
// we may inspect the company variable here
if (company!=null)
{
    write ('Company name is:');
    write(company.name);
}
```

6.6 Guarantee operator precedence

As we find ourselves switching between platforms, we will find certain languages work one way, and other languages work in another. As the number of platforms we work on grows, it gets increasingly hard to remember all the quirks of any specific platform. As such, it pays off to write code in such a way that there is no room for misunderstanding. Consider, for example, the following valid Visual Basic statement:

```
if a is not b then statement
```

Although this is pretty readable for native English speakers, logically speaking it doesn't make a lot of sense. In most programming languages, the not operator has precedence over most other operators. Most programming languages would treat the statement above as

```
if ((a) is (not b)) then statement
```

Most likely, this is not what the programmer intended to write, as it checks whether variable a is of the same data type as the result of the expression (not b). Most likely, b and (not b) are of the same data type, causing statement to always be executed. To avoid any possible confusion caused by these differences, we best write down the statement in a way that more explicitly shows what we intend to say, regardless of programming language:

```
if (not (a is b)) then statement
```

In pretty much any programming language, the use of brackets helps to make sure that the expression is evaluated in the order that we intended[14]. As a result, there is also less room for misinterpretation of our intentions; not only by the compiler, but also our fellow programmers. In the above IF statement, the outermost brackets are added because in C-like languages, they are required to detect the start and end of the expression. As they do no harm in other languages, we might as well get used to including them.

Along the same lines, always explicitly use compound statements. The following code is open for multiple interpretations[15]:

```
if (expr)
    // expression is valid
    do_something();
```

A programming language might, in theory, interpret this as follows:

```
if (expr)
{
    // expression is valid
}
do_something();
```

---

14 In some languages such as assembly and Forth, it is the programmer who has to provide operations in the correct order.

15 This is a non-issue in the Python programming language, where compound statements are grouped together by their indentation.

But the programmer probably meant:

```
if (expr)
{
    // expression is valid
    do_something();
}
```

When we make our intentions explicit through the notation that we use, there will no longer be room for misunderstanding, either from co-workers or from the compiler we use. Also, with the curly brackets are already in place, we can no longer forget adding them later on. As a result, there is less chance to break the code when we add one or more statements to the THEN or ELSE branch of an IF statement.

6.7 Keep loops in the correct order

There are cases when it looks like the only way to keep a loop clean is to put it in reverse order. An example is when we want to read and process a file until a certain character is found. Some instructors would write a piece of code for this as follows:

```
function readfile(File file)
{
    char invalue;
    invalue=file.read();
    while (invalue != TERMINATION_CHAR)
    {
        process(invalue);
        invalue=file.read();
    }
}
```

Some drawbacks of writing code like this are:

- The `file.read()` code is duplicated, which potentially increases maintenance;

- The contents of the loop seem to be in reverse order (processing a value, then reading one);

- Iterations require the result of the previous iteration. This indicates that the code is not context free; it introduces a memory effect. This means that if we wanted to skip a few iterations for efficiency reasons, it would be likely that the code would stop working.

Ideally, the block of code inside the loop can be verified for correctness by itself, without needing to look at the code that is outside the loop in another scope. Because of this, it would seem more logical to write the code as follows:

```
function readfile(File file)
{
    while (true)
    {
        char invalue=file.read();
        if (invalue==TERMINATION_CHAR)
        {
            break;
        }
        process(invalue);
    }
}
```

Functionally, the two snippets are equal, but the latter code no longer requires code duplication, reducing maintenance. As variable invalue is only defined inside the loop, it can have no influence outside that scope, reducing the possibility of bugs. The code can now also be read front-to-back, which is not only more intuitive than the former solution, it would also allow us to move the loop contents into a stateless function.

Another possibility is to use a do..while (or repeat..until) loop. This would have the benefit of automatically getting into the correct order. The drawback however is that it needs to check invalue twice: once to see if it needs processing, and once to see if the loop needs to be iterated again. By interrupting the loop with a break statement, this is no longer needed. We also see that the difference between the two types of loop (while vs. repeat..until) is essentially eliminated.

6.8 Prevent wasting processing power

The following code shows a case of an often seen programming technique which unnecessarily wastes processing power. It is frequently caused by bug fixes and changing requirements that are implemented in a hurry.

```
bool hasNullObject(Object object1,
                   Object object2,
                   Object object3)
{
    bool hasNull=false;
    if (object1==null)
    {
        hasNull=true;
    }
    else
    {
        if (object2==null)
        {
            hasNull=true;
        }
    }
    /* Bugfix by Bob, check object3 */
    if (object3==null)
    {
        hasNull=true;
    }
    return hasNull;
}
```

What happens here? If any of the precondition checks fails, the return value is already known. Nothing ever changes it anymore, but we will only find out and know for sure after reading the rest of the function. After all, after the ELSE branch of the IF statement closes, in theory the function might still change its mind.

So we read the rest of the function as well, only to find out we wasted valuable reading time because the return value isn't changed once it is set.

But that's not all. In the example above, we don't only waste time of the code reader, but also processing power. The value of the return variable is never changed anymore once it is set, yet we force the computer to do more comparisons, wasting processor resources. For clarity, let us also show this in a PSD (Program Structure Diagram):

bool hasNullObject(Object object1,Object object2, Object object3)		
hasNull=false;		
object1==null?		
true	false	
	object2==null?	
	true	false
hasNull=true;	hasNull=true;	/* else statement is empty. Did we forget something? */
object3==null?		
true	false	
hasNull=true;	/* else statement is empty. Did we forget something? */	
return hasNull;		

The PSD didn't add a lot of clarity, did it? This is what happens when a bug fix is carelessly slapped at the bottom of the function. The result is that the function no longer clearly shows all possible code paths. But look what happens if we refactor the code to return as soon as the return value is known:

```
bool hasNullObject(Object object1,
                   Object object2,
                   Object object3)
{
    if (object1==null)
    {
        return true;
    }
    if (object2==null)
    {
        return true;
    }
    if (object3==null)
    {
        return true;
    }
    return false;
}
```

By returning from the function as soon as possible, we've obtained code that executes faster and that gives bugs less place to hide. We also save ourselves a (marginal) bit of memory by no longer needing the return variable. In addition, it will be easier to optimize further, should this be important; we can simply swap around IF statements if one object is null more frequently than others. The PSD suddenly appears beautifully structured:

```
function hasNullObject(Object object1,Object
object2, Object object3) returns bool
```

object1==null?		
true	false	
	object2==null?	
	true	false
		object3==null?
		true	false
return true;		return false;

Obviously, in the latter case, the programmer had a more defined thought about which return value was to be given when. In the PSD, in a single glance we can see in which case each result is obtained, and this can also easily be traced back bottom-up to the condition that returned that result. Intuitively, it will be easier to proof the correctness of the code, because we can instantly see all 4 possible code paths created by the conditions. When drawing a PSD such as the one above, we may switch around the `true` and `false` branches to have the code that actually does something on one side, and the branches that do nothing on the other.

It should also be noted that in the PSD we can do something that code doesn't allow us to do, which is to let multiple `IF` statements share the same `THEN` branch. This show us that a PSD code editor would potentially allow us to have more control over code duplication than a traditional text editor. Likewise, if the programming language of our choice provides us with some way to define a termination clause for our functions, we will have more control over code duplication.

Some programmers prefer single-exit code rather than early-exit code. That's fine; the above PSD suits both notations equally well. To turn the above PSD into a true single-exit PSD, however, a few minor changes are needed:

- Instead of writing `return true;` or `return false;` we write `result=true;` or `result=false;`

- At the end of our code we write `return result;`

- The resulting single-exit PSD and code look as follows (in essence structurally identical to the one before):

function hasNullObject(Object object1,Object object2, Object object3) returns bool				
object1==null?				
true	**false**			
	object2==null?			
	true	**false**		
		object3==null?		
		true	**false**	
result=true;			result=false;	
return result;				

```
bool hasNullObject(Object object1,Object object2,
                   Object object3)
{
    bool result;
    if (object1==null)
    {
        result=true;
    }
    else
    {
        if (object2==null)
        {
            result=true;
        }
        else
        {
            if (object3==null)
            {
                result=true;
            }
            else
            {
                result=false;
            }
        }
    }
    return result;
}
```

People that like to write single-exit code probably like this last piece code better than the early-exit code. As mentioned before, when we compare the PSD of single-exit code to the PSD of multiple-exit code, we will see that there is no vital structural difference between them. The only difference is the `return` statement in the end; either style of writing code results in the same semantic structure. There are some benefits to either style.

The benefit of early-exit code is that it shows the result of both branches of an IF statement in the smallest possible scope. To explain this, consider the following two snippets of code:

- Single exit:

```
if (a==null)
{
    result=true;
}
else
{
    /* 1000 lines of code
       (that might, or not, overrule result
        due to programmer Bob slapping a
        bug fix in the bottom of the function)
    */
}
return result;
```

- Early exit:

```
if (a==null)
{
    return true;
}
/* 1000 lines of code
   (that can never overrule result)
*/
```

These two pieces of code may or may not be semantically equal. Specifically, in the first code snippet, will the value of variable result still change? I can't tell unless I follow the flow of another 1000 lines of code.

The early-exit code answers this question by immediately closing the scope of the IF statement. By keeping minimal extent, it is instantly obvious that the answer is, "No, the return value will not change anymore".

Of course, it is best not to let a function grow to 1000 lines, and split code up into smaller functions before we face these problems.

Previously we have seen that keeping the smallest possible extent helps improve modularity of our code, which in turn allows such code to more easily be abstracted into functions. This suggests that early-exit code is a better choice for producing modular, low-maintenance code, while making it easier to write structured code that is easy to read.

In contrast, there is also some substance to the claims that early-exit code will make our code more sensitive to bugs, harder to troubleshoot and more likely to introduce code duplication.

The following example will demonstrate the issues that we must be aware of, should we choose to write early-exit code:

```
function write_something_to_file() returns bool
{
    Fhandle handle=fopen("filename.txt","w");
    if (handle==null)
    {
        return false;
    }

    bool canwrite=success_write_to_file(handle);
    if (!(canwrite))
    {
        fclose(handle); // cleanup code
        return false;
    }

    canwrite=can_write_more(handle);
    if (!(canwrite))
    {
        fclose(handle); // cleanup code
        return false;
    }

    fclose(handle); // cleanup code
    return true; // successful termination
}
```

The code attempts to write something to a file, and includes both error trapping and clean-up code.

Using early-exit coding makes it necessary to duplicate code to perform clean-up, which is a bad thing. If the clean-up code changes, we will need to change it everywhere (which implies increased maintenance), or else we introduce a bug. When attempting to troubleshoot this bug, we will find that there is no single exit-point where we can check the post-conditions of the function (as the function has multiple return statements).

This can be resolved by putting the clean-up code in a function or by using the `try..finally` construct that some programming languages offer, although this will have a (small) performance penalty. In such cases, single-exit code may offer a more elegant solution, as we will see in the following example:

```
function write_something_to_file() returns bool
{
    Fhandle handle=fopen("filename.txt","w");
    bool result=false;
    if (handle!=null)
    {
        bool canwrite
            =success_write_to_file(handle);

        if (canwrite)
        {
            canwrite=can_write_more(handle);
            if (canwrite)
            {
                result=true;
            }
        }
        else
        {
            result=false;
        }
        fclose(handle); // only 1x cleanup code
    }
    /* we can check all postconditions here*/
    return result;
}
```

No code is duplicated in this example, and all postconditions can be verified in a single location. We should keep in mind that we have solved one problem, but not without a few trade-offs.

Introducing the `result` variable makes this code use more memory. Also, assigning a value to this variable will have a slight performance impact. The extent of each individual statement is bigger, which implies reduced modularity.

In early-exit functions, we have to figure out where we need to make changes before we can make them. Single-exit functions, in contrast, allow us to simply add code at the end of the function. This can be perceived as a benefit, but carelessness in doing is the main cause of the structural issues and performance loss demonstrated earlier in this chapter.

Overall, the structure of the code in the last two examples is virtually identical[16]. This identical structure shows us that either fragment of code isn't better than the other, which is similar to the two code snippets in chapter **Avoid GOTO** (see page 101).

Hopefully, after reading this chapter, you will be able to recognize when to use single-exit, and when to use early-exit coding style.

If you deal with single-exit code, I hope that after reading this chapter, you will be able to recognize which code can safely be added to the end of a function, and which code will cause problems in the structure of your code.

16Drawing the corresponding PSD is left as an exercise to the reader.

6.9 Put code in the most efficient order

Sometimes we see code that seems in internal conflict with itself: it performs some operations, only to discard the effort a bit later on and overrule it by other operations. Such awful code can often be improved dramatically by reordering the order of execution. An example of such code is the following:

```
function return_a_value(bool mustreturnthird,
                  bool mustreturndefault)
{
    // return the third value, default or a sum
    int defaultvalue = lookup_default();
    int firstvalue = lookup_first();
    int secondvalue = lookup_second();
    int resultvalue = firstvalue + secondvalue;

    if (mustreturnthird)
    {
        int thirdvalue = lookup_third_value();
        resultvalue = thirdvalue;
    }

    if(mustreturndefault)
    {
        resultvalue = defaultvalue;
    }
    return resultvalue;
}
```

It is possible to rewrite this code to prevent unnecessary operations. Like tying shoe laces, it is easier to do it than to explain how, but let me give it a shot.

First of all, there are a few rules that we will follow when rewriting the above code:

1. We only make changes that maintain the meaning of the code. Otherwise we will break the code.

2. We postpone operations until they are needed. This prevents wasting processor resources.

3. Results that are overridden move down; results that are not overridden move up. As a result, we will no longer need to override any results.

When we look at the former code, we see that the result of the lookups is only used conditionally.

In this case, postponing the lookups until their result is used (rule 2) does not alter the meaning of the code (rule 1), so we move the lookups down to just before where their result is required.

After following the second rule, the code will look as follows:

```
function return_a_value(bool mustreturnthird,
                        bool mustreturndefault)
{
    // return the third value, default or a sum
    int firstvalue = lookup_first();
    int secondvalue = lookup_second();
    int resultvalue = firstvalue + secondvalue;
    resultvalue = firstvalue + secondvalue;

    if (mustreturnthird)
    {
        int thirdvalue = lookup_third_value();
        resultvalue = thirdvalue;
    }
    if(mustreturndefault)
    {
        // Default lookup is moved down to here
        int defaultvalue=lookup_default();
        resultvalue = defaultvalue;
    }
    return resultvalue;
}
```

Now for the third rule. The only result that is not overridden is that of the last if statement. By adapting an early-exit strategy (temporarily, if you prefer) we can rewrite the last snippet of code without changing its meaning:

```
if (mustreturndefault)
{
    int defaultvalue = lookup_default();
    resultvalue = defaultvalue;
    return resultvalue;
}
return resultvalue;
```

The result of the last if statement is never overridden. Because of this, we can move it up all the way to the start of the function. The return statement we added helps us to preserve the meaning of the code.

```
function return_a_value(bool mustreturnthird,
                        bool mustreturndefault)
{
    // return the third value, default or a sum
    if(mustreturndefault)
    {
        int defaultvalue = lookup_default();
        resultvalue = defaultvalue;
        return resultvalue;
    }
    int firstvalue = lookup_first();
    int secondvalue = lookup_second();
    int resultvalue = firstvalue+secondvalue;

    if (mustreturnthird)
    {
        int thirdvalue=lookup_third_value();
        resultvalue = thirdvalue;
    }
    return resultvalue;
}
```

Likewise, the last if statement overrides the result value calculated before it (however, it will not override our first if statement anymore due to the return statement). We can also add a return statement to it, which once again leaves the meaning of the last snippet of code intact:

```
if (mustreturnthird)
{
    int thirdvalue=lookup_third_value();
    resultvalue = thirdvalue;
    return resultvalue;
}
return resultvalue;
```

Then, we can move the `if` statement up (until *after* the previous statement that we moved, otherwise we would change the meaning of the code):

```
function return_a_value(bool mustreturnthird,
                        bool mustreturndefault)
{
    // return the third value, default or a sum
    if (mustreturndefault)
    {
        int defaultvalue=lookup_default();
        resultvalue = defaultvalue;
        return resultvalue;
    }
    if (mustreturnthird)
    {
        int thirdvalue=lookup_third_value();
        resultvalue = thirdvalue;
        return resultvalue;
    }
    int firstvalue=lookup_first();
    int secondvalue=lookup_second();
    int resultvalue = firstvalue + secondvalue;
    return resultvalue;
}
```

The code now no longer overrides any results, so we are practically done refactoring it. As the variable resultvalue is no longer needed, we can eliminate it. This will in turn show us that most other variables are no longer needed either, so we eliminate these as well. Here is the resulting code:

```
function return_a_value(bool mustreturnthird,
                        bool mustreturndefault)
{
    // return the third value, default or a sum
    if (mustreturndefault)
    {
        return lookup_default();
    }
    if (mustreturnthird)
    {
        return lookup_third_value();
    }
    return lookup_first() + lookup_second();
}
```

We have eliminated all unnecessary variables from the code. This helps guarantee that the various pieces of code will not have a memory effect that may influence the other pieces of code.

The resulting code is shorter, clearer and will no longer performs unneeded assignments and lookups. We may verify that the result is indeed compatible with the original function by writing a unit test.

If you prefer to write single-exit functions, you may want to turn the code into its single-exit equivalent by assigning to a result value rather than exiting, which will render the following result:

```
function return_a_value(bool mustreturnthird,
                        bool mustreturndefault)
{
    // return the third value, default or a sum
    int resultvalue;
    if(mustreturndefault)
    {
        resultvalue = lookup_default();
    }
    else
    {
        if (mustreturnthird)
        {
            resultvalue = lookup_third_value();
        }
        else
        {
            resultvalue=lookup_first()
                        +lookup_second();
        }
    }
    return resultvalue;
}
```

However, the added value of this last transformation is marginal. The extra assignment will make the code less efficient, and subsequent code reordering will be more tricky. Also, writing down code this way will make it more likely to end up with code that has the same problems as the code that we just refactored.

We should recognize that refactoring code implies the risk that we may introduce bugs. Especially functions that have side effects or that are not referentially transparent increase this risk.

If, for instance, function `lookup_default()` opens a file that is required by the other `lookup()` functions, the rewritten version of the function will no longer work, because some functions in the original code depended on a side effect of other functions. In such cases, it is better to address the referential transparency of the called functions first.

When refactoring code, beware of functions and procedures that use global variables; these are likely to be functions with side effects. Functions that are especially suspect to have side effects are functions that are called without parameters, but that do return a value. This is often an indication that global variables are in use. In the former code, the `lookup()` functions would be up for inspection before we would start refactoring the code.

Finally, it is a good idea to unit test the refactored function, to make sure we didn't break anything. If an official unit test doesn't exist yet for the old function, a simple way to perform the unit test is by keeping a copy of the old function before refactoring, and calling it from the rewritten function to compare and match the result. If the functions give equal results for all possible inputs, the unit test has succeeded and we can discard the old function.

6.10 Start and finish in the same scope

When writing code that creates objects, we should be aware that objects can either be created on the stack or on the heap. When objects are created on the stack, any object-oriented language will automatically call their destructor when the function terminates. This will help prevent memory leaks. However, it makes it risky to write code that creates objects and attempts to return them to another scope, such as the following:

```
LinkedList create_linked_list(int numberofnodes)
{
    /* create a linked list with the
       given number of nodes */
    int i;
    LinkedList mylist;
    for (i=1; i<=numberofnodes;i++)
    {
        ListNode * mylistnode=new ListNode();
        mylist.Add(mylistnode);
    }
    return mylist;
}
```

When the above function terminates, variable `mylist` will go out of scope and its destructor will be called. However, the pointer value used beneath the surface may not be reset. As a result, the list may seem available, but get corrupted as the application runs.

A compiler could detect this and complain about it, but not all compilers will. By creating and destructing objects in the same scope, this risk is avoided. The above function could be rewritten as:

```
LinkedList init_linked_list(LinkedList mylist,
                                 int numberofnodes)
{
    /* initialize the linked list with the
       given number of nodes */
    int i;
    for (i=1; i<=numberofnodes;i++)
    {
        ListNode * mylistnode=new ListNode();
        mylist.Add(mylistnode);
    }
    return mylist; // destructor won't be called
}
```

The actual allocating of the `mylist` object is then done by the caller:

```
int main()
{
    LinkedList *mylist;
    mylist=new LinkedList(); // stub for list

    mylist=init_linked_list(mylist,5);
    use_the_list_as_we_please(mylist);

    delete mylist; /* delete and new called
                      in the same function */
}
```

In this new and improved version, the linked list is created in the same scope in which it is destructed, which at least allow us to check for memory leaks more easily. Although returning `mylist` from the function is not needed when passing the object by reference, it makes it clear to other programmers that the list is manipulated.

Obviously, in the case of object-oriented programming, allocation of resources will often be done in the constructor (or even better, in an initialization function called *after* successful object creation), while clean-up of the same resources is done in the object destructor. Although this is technically not the same scope, it serves the same purpose.

Finally, this technique is also useful for other operations that have a clearly defined start, middle and end, such as opening and closing files, setting up and closing database connections, and so on.

6.11 Static vs. Dynamic programming

In creating applications, we often have the choice between implementing something statically in code, or to do the same by dynamically creating the same effect in runtime. This is possibly most obvious in creating user interfaces creation, but it applies more general to code generators as well.

We can spend endless hours fine tuning a user interface, by drawing buttons and other controls on a form, only to find out the result is not readily adaptable. However, usually it pays off to go the extra mile and learn how to generate the same user interface in runtime. This will give a great deal of added flexibility in the long run. Still, generating everything in runtime also has a few drawbacks. The following comparison chart outlines the benefits and drawbacks of statically predefining code vs. generating it dynamically, in runtime.

Statically coded user interface	*User interface dynamically generated in runtime*
Initially easier to implement: For instance, by dragging and dropping buttons onto a form.	Initially harder to implement: requires knowledge on how to generate user interface elements, how to position them, how to control their style and how to link them to code.
Static: User interface always looks the same. Will sometimes require us to introduce logical limitations (e.g. a maximum of 4 children per person).	Dynamic: We can be presented with just the relevant interface elements at any time. Will allow us to completely bypass logical limitations.
Allows us to stay ignorant of the inner workings of the framework used.	Will give us in-depth knowledge of the user interface framework used.
Not customizable by end users.	Potentially highly customizable by end users.

Statically coded user interface	*User interface dynamically generated in runtime*
A change in layout (such as font) means manually updating all relevant user interface element (which may be a big task). Recompiling may be required to reflect the changes.	Little work to maintain: Allows us to create a data driven user interface. A change in layout (e.g. font) only needs to be done in 1 place, as the user interface is re-generated in runtime. Changes are reflected without need for recompiling.
Typically serves one medium only (e.g. screen).	Because of being data driven, may serve various platforms (screen, Braille terminal, web browser, etc.)

When we use code generators, a similar situation applies. There are code generators that generate static code once, which still needs fine-tuning by hand. These code generators do not allow us to bypass their inner workings, so we have to adapt our way of working to them. This is fine as long as we actually only need a one-time code generation, such as is the case with generating an application framework using a wizard.

However, we will not be able to maintain our code with the same code generator. As a result, we better get things right the first time, or else we will be stuck with extra maintenance.

On the other hand, there are code generators that allow us to maintain the entire project from within them. Though it may be a bit bold to consider them as code generators, most compilers fall into this category. Likewise, any tool that we use to convert a text file to code written in the language of our choice, we use such a generator.

Any time we need to generate code, we just re-generate all code, and things will be fine. As a result we may keep an entire project in such an environment. Ideally the environment is aware of its own limitations, allowing us to bypass them.

In case of compilers, for example, this bypass can be provided by an in-line assembler or the possibility to link external libraries to our code. The original ANSI Pascal language failed in this respect, whereas in Borland Turbo Pascal this was addressed.

When we write a code generator ourselves, it is worth the effort to have it generate a comment in the header of the target code. This comment should state that the code is generated, and also how and where any edit operations should take place.

This page intentionally left blank

Chapter 7

Make your work user friendly

The term 'user friendly' is, unfortunately, subjective. A good, widely accepted definition doesn't really exist. A program that is called user friendly by one person is a mystery to another. Because of this, a functional specification mentioning that a program should be 'user friendly' is not specific enough to define project scope.

However, the term 'user friendly' has been increasingly used to indicate the usability of a program. There are several things you can do that will help in making it more obvious how to use your programs, and several other things that will make your program more pleasant to use. These techniques will be discussed on the pages that follow.

7.1 Limit user input

Limiting user input is one of the most effective best practices in creating user friendly software. The less users can do wrong to start with, the fewer conditions you will need to check in your code. Instead of checking if user input is correct after it is given by the user, make sure they can not possibly give wrong input.

From the perspective of the user, this will allow him or her to move around the program without being confronted with error messages all the time saying that (s)he has done something wrong. If the user is simply unable to give wrong input, that will definitely make them feel a lot smarter!

If you thought that computers like the Apple Macintosh or Windows machines were designed only to make things easier to the user, think again. The implications actually reach much further from a programming point of view, because of the deliberate limitations introduced by graphical user interfaces.

In a command-line interface, programmers would need to filter all kinds of incorrect input; in a graphical environment, we can simply prevent users from giving the wrong commands. For example, a date picker will guarantee that the user won't make formatting errors when entering dates. Other wrong input, such as mouse clicks on areas of the screen that do not contain any controls, can simply be ignored. As a result, less code needs to be written.

7.2 Provide visual clues

Users will not be able to read your mind about fancy key/mouse combinations that they need to use to get things done. The user can not be expected to guess that the F4 button needs to be pressed to open a file, or that pressing control-shift-escape will cause a network meltdown if so desired.

Give your users visual clues about how to use the program[17]. If first-time users need to be explained that they have to press a certain key to use the program, you may want to reconsider that part of the user interface.

A common visual clue in web forms is marking a text field in a certain way (often a little star), if the user is obliged to enter data in it. By itself this does not explain anything; as such, it is also useful to add a little explanation about this mark on the screen.

If you want to insist on having the user work with a certain key/ mouse combination to obtain the desired behaviour, you might use a tool tip. For instance, if they hover over a control that can be control-clicked, display a tool tip that says "Ctrl-click this item for this-or-that behaviour". The same goes for double-clicking items, click-and-hold and drag-and-drop. The more clear a program is visually, the less room there is for confusion.

Grey out screen elements that can not be clicked, or hide them altogether. If a button is disabled and greyed out, a user may wonder "Why is this button grey? I need to click it, how can I enable it?"

---

17 Of course for non-visual systems such as automated answering machines, visual clues won't do, so give helpful indications otherwise.

We can help the user by giving a visual clue saying "this button will be enabled as soon as you do this-or-that". This clue could for example be given as a simple text message on screen.

Additional information may be given when an action may confuse the user. An example of this is deleting shortcuts from the Windows desktop. In the past, Windows would ask for confirmation as follows: "Do you wish to delete 'Program'?"

This would confuse especially semi-informed users that knew they might lose the program altogether. In more recent versions, the users are given more confidence, simply because the message has changed a bit. It now says something along the lines of "Are you sure you want to remove 'Program' from the desktop? This will not uninstall the program." This gives the user the confidence to proceed.

Finally, when using icons for visual clues, use images that depict what you intend to say in a language independent manner. A picture of a block of wood is probably not going to be understood as 'log' icon in most languages.

7.3 Prevent raising errors unnecessarily

When a program requires a user to enter a phone number, we can expect the user to enter all kinds of characters: spaces, brackets, slashes, dashes, and so on.

Should the user enter unwanted characters, we can respond by giving an error "You entered an invalid phone number, a phone number should be formatted as follows...".

As user input should be filtered before use anyway, it is friendlier to let our program filter the input for unwanted contents *before* checking if it is valid. In this manner, we will not make the user feel stupid for our own lack of sensibility.

If a field normally would require some formatting such as punctuation or dashes (such as in a date field), see if it is possible to accept input in such a way that formatting is no longer important. Perhaps dashes be omitted and added at the right spots later on; or perhaps the values could be entered as multiple fields so that the formatting no longer matters.

Or perhaps the problem could have been prevented altogether by limiting the user input (as mentioned before) by means of a pop-up dialog, a wizard or an input field that only accepts numbers.

7.4 Use blocking errors sparingly

A very effective way to drive your users up the wall is to raise an error as soon as the slightest mistake is made, and insist that this error be corrected at the second that it occurs. Examples of this are input fields that capture the cursor until correct input is given, or blocking validations that are performed on every key-press. As sometimes validations depend on a combination of factors, it may be the actual mistake isn't in the current input field.

Apart from causing a considerable amount of irritation, early blocking errors increase the risk that your user interface presents the users with an error situation that can not be resolved by them.

Instead, trust that the user will get back to those errors to correct them. Often, in your system there will be a point where a series of validations can be performed at once. At that moment, the user can be presented with a list of errors. This is also more pleasant to the user than presenting just one error at a time, which may cause the user to sigh, "What *else* have I done wrong?"

To help the users enter data correctly, we may make them aware of errors in an early stage by giving a non-blocking visual clue. If we have a visual user interface, we could for instance display a red X next to an input field, while the content of the field is incorrect. This will not prevent the users to move around the user interface, but help them in fixing any problems.

7.5 Value the efforts of your users

Imagine a user that has just spent fifteen minutes filling out a complex form. After submitting it, the system shows an error message:

```
You  forgot  to  enter  the  field  'Middle  name'.
Press a key to try again.
```

After doing as requested, the system presents the user with an empty form, and the user has to re-enter all data, *including the data that was previously entered correctly*. The problem is twofold: Not only was the effort of the user wasted, but there is no guarantee that all data will be entered correctly the second time around. The users of such a system are in for a lot of frustration. The described system would be much more friendly if all correctly entered data was restored into the correction form, so that users could limit themselves to correcting mistakes.

If you can prevent unnecessary actions, this may also be perceived as positive. Many programs nowadays show dialog boxes along with a checkbox saying "Don't show this message again" or "Remember this answer", which will save the user unneeded frustration and actions in the future.

Along the same lines, if a program runs into a fatal error, you can save your users a lot of work by saving a crash dump before exiting, which then can be used for recovery the next time the program is opened. An alternative approach to this is to build in an auto-save feature which periodically saves the work of the users.

7.6 Let error messages help the user

When the input can not be limited by means of input or selections, we will have to raise an error to the user if a field validation failed. If you have a form with many fields to validate, it is probably friendlier to collect errors and list them, than to pop-up an error dialog for each individual error. When you really need to give error messages, make sure that they will be useful, preferably both to yourself as a programmer and to the user.

To the user, an error message such as

```
The calculated value is too high.
```

will possibly not be very informative on a form with multiple calculated values. The following alternative is a lot more useful:

```
Based on your salary data, the calculated price of
150000 dollars for the selected article 'Lamborghini
Murcielago' is too high for you to pay in cash.
Correct your salary data, choose a cheaper product or
get a loan.
```

The extra clarity is not just a result of being more verbose, but a result of giving additional information about the cause of the error and possible solutions to resolve it. Optionally, we may create a wizard to assist the user in resolving the problem.

7.7 Guide the user in providing input

Despite our best efforts, users may enter incorrect data due to typos. To reduce the number of errors caused by this, it is possible to incorporate some type of checksum. An example of this is the LUHN-10 check on credit card numbers. Although a correct checksum is no guarantee for a valid number, at least an incorrect checksum guarantees that the number is invalid, which allows reducing invalid input by 90% without ever needing to consult a database of valid credit card numbers.

Although this works well to distinguish between valid and invalid keys, it is not a lot of help for free-form input, in which all input is technically correct.

In such systems, we may offer guidance by providing the user with alternatives. Various search engines offer an alternative for search terms that we type in by asking: "Did you mean *<alternative term>*?"

One way to do this is by assigning scores based on exact spelling. Another way, which is used in governmental databases, is to employ a soundex algorithm to allow the call center employees to find back data based on their phonetic sound. A soundex algorithm works by assigning equal codes to letters that represent similar sounds[18]. As a result, the correct information can be found even if the person answering the phone didn't get the spelling right.

---

18 The original soundex algorithm is based on the pronunciation rules of the English language and may not work well for other languages. See 'The Art of Computer Programming' by Donald Knuth.

7.8 Prevent duplicate data entry

Some time ago I had to make a phone call to my energy supplier. I was directed to an automated menu in which I had to enter my client number, so I did. The call was then transferred to a lady who handled the call. Her first question was: "What is your client number?" This puzzled me. As the system wouldn't transfer the call without asking and verifying my client number, why was that question necessary?

From a user perspective, duplicate data entry such as which I faced when calling my energy supplier is a minor inconvenience, but nothing more than that.

In information systems, duplicate data entry can result in bigger problems. Manually entered data is sensitive to typos. As a result, two copies of what should be identical information can end up contradicting each other.

Having to enter the same data twice causes a direct loss of productivity (because the same work has to be done twice), but eventually an additional loss of productivity caused by having to figure out which of the two pieces of information is real, and to set straight any mistakes.

In exceptional cases, duplicate data entry has its uses, to guarantee high integrity data input. The requirement to enter a password twice to change it is a good example of this. Of course, although the password is entered twice, only one password is stored (after the entered passwords are verified to match), so there is no doubt about which password is the correct one.

7.9 Make your program look familiar

When you take a look at two different spreadsheet programs, or two different mail programs, or two different web browsers, you will often find striking similarities. In fact, when observing two entirely different programs, such as a web browser and a word processor, equally striking similarities can be seen: A title bar, a menu stating `File Edit View Tools Window Help`, an icon bar beneath it, a status bar on the bottom.

Repeating this structure rather than inventing one of your own will likely help you save time in designing a user interface. To save time, leave out some elements, if you wish. A structure like the one mentioned will help you in your design, and it will also help the user in using your program.

A bit more experienced user already knows that it is common practice to save a file with the `File->Save` menu, before having seen your program. If your program meets such expectations, bonus points to you.

There is no official standard for custom-built financial applications or GUI front-ends for huge databases, but a structure similar to a mail program seems to be suitable for most software. A folder bar (or navigation pane) on the left, a list of records on the right. Double-clicking a record opens a form to edit that record. Meanwhile, the top of the screen shows a row of icons or buttons that allow the user to perform common actions, such as saving the data.

By observing an email application, you will see that a lot of search functionality is made redundant by the fact that you can sort the contents of the mailbox by clicking column headers. To find an email, you will probably start out by selecting a specific mail folder, followed by clicking the column header to sort the mail overview by date, subject or sender. Failing that, you use the search functionality, which will scan the actual contents of the records.

7.10 Use information analysis in UI design

By the state of a user interface, we can usually tell a lot about how well designed a program is underneath. This little chapter will make clear why: information analysis not only has its benefits in designing databases, but also can have a lot of impact in user interface design.

Imagine we are creating a database system that allows us to create client records and contracts. We perform a quick information analysis and find out that a contract must belong to a single client, whereas a client can have 0, 1 or many contracts. Based on this, we find the database may contain the following tables:

Table contract

field name	*field type*	*NULL?*
contract_id	primary key	no
client_id	foreign key referencing field client_id in table clients	no
contract_content	blob	yes

Table client

field name	*field type*	*NULL?*
client_id	primary key	no
client_name	varchar(127)	no
client_dateofbirth	date	yes

By looking at these tables, we can tell that a client can exist without a contract, but a contract can not exist without a client.

If we want to make things easy for ourselves, we base our user interface on the data structure of our database. This implies that it makes more sense to choose the client in the contract screen than to create contracts in the client screen: there is nothing about contracts in the clients table, so there will be nothing about contracts on the client screen.

This will help us keep our client screen re-usable for other systems, with or without contracts (see also: **Write knowledge-free functions**, page 244). It will also help keep the user interface of the client screen clean and simple. If we allow a contract button on the client screen, imagine what will happen if client data would be related to dozens of other types of data: The client screen would possibly be cluttered with dozens of buttons and look more like a space ship than like a client form.

In our lean and mean user interface, our user happily navigates to the contract list and clicks `New contract`. An empty contract is displayed. Only now our user realizes that the client data doesn't exist yet.

Our user has to perform quite a few actions to resolve this:

- cancel the contract and navigate back to the contract list,

- click the client navigation button,

- click the 'create client' button

- enter client data and save it,

- navigate back to the client list,

- click the contracts navigation button,

- and re-create the new contract.

Obviously this is not very efficient, and we will be able to predict various complaints from our user. We can resolve this without cluttering the client screen by allowing users to create clients from within the contract screen. In the same situation as above, our user now will do the following:

- click the 'create client' button (or perhaps to keep the user interface clean, all client functions are available via the 'choose client' button)

- enter client data and save it

- close the client screen

Our user can now continue writing the contract (rather than starting over as before - which might have been a reason for lost productivity) and client data may even already have been filled in automatically into the contract when closing the client screen. This makes the user interface much more effective, without cluttering it with lots of buttons.

As a bonus, next time we need a client screen, there is a chance that we can reuse the one we designed before.

7.11 Don't irritate the user

While the user is performing a task, our program may perform some background processing. Perhaps at some point, we will want to bring something to the attention of the user, or while the user is typing a search query, we have found a partial result.

A program can be considered irritating if it interrupts what the user is doing, and demanding other action before allowing the user to continue the previous task. An example of this is stealing focus while the user is typing something. Imagine a spell checker that would pop up a dialog box demanding correction after every misspelled word – how irritating would that be? By this example, the solution is also obvious: Display a discreet visual clue, and the user will be able to respond at the best suited moment. Flashing the task bar is already a big improvement over stealing focus.

Even if you don't steal focus, effects such as sounds, blinking, overly bright colours and animations can be distracting. When you must add them, allow the user to turn them off.

When a program changes the input of the user, while the user is working with that input, this invariably leads to unwanted changes once in a while. This too should be avoided, or at least the user should be given a way to disable this behaviour. A particularly irritating example is an auto-complete algorithm that will complete any incomplete word after each key-press – even when the backspace key is used, effectively rendering the backspace key unusable.

7.12 Don't confuse end users with jargon

Not all your users are as bright as you are. Using a lot of technical terms in your applications is a sure-fire way to confuse some of your users, so please try to avoid overly technical terms.

But users also don't like to be treated like four-year-olds.

Sometimes it is not possible or impractical to avoid jargon. In such cases, it helps to keep the following in mind. When faced with something they don't understand, some users prefer to stay ignorant, while others want an explanation.

Hide technical information from the first group; provide a way to make this information available to the second group (perhaps by clicking a button labelled 'Advanced...'). Include a textual explanation, if you want.

7.13 Visit the hall of fame and shame

User interface design can be a very creative activity. A bit too creative, at times. Sometimes learning by counter-example works better than learning by example, so start up your favourite search engine, search for "user interface hall of shame", and have a good laugh.

7.14 Perform usability tests

Finally, have a few people that are not familiar with your application try to perform some common tasks with it. This will help you find out which parts of your user interface still need further attention.

Chapter 8

Make your work 'programmer friendly'

The amount of time needed for another programmer to be able to start working on your code is a good indicator of its clarity. If it takes more than a few weeks to get familiar enough with a project to become productive, this is a strong indication that something is wrong. By adapting a transparent working methodology, other programmers will more easily adapt to your code, your code will be more portable, and bugs have less place to hide. You know that you've run into a master programmer when an extensive system written by that programmer doesn't *seem* to be complex.

The code is modular and full of useful comments, but is quite readable even without them. Here and there the code contains pointers to the paper documentation- or the documentation is part of the code itself.

Code of a master programmer distinguishes itself by its absence of implicit information. Explanations are right there in the code itself, not just in the head of the programmer.

We can come a step closer to being a master programmer by being explicit about what our code does and how it works; by writing code that is no more complex than absolutely necessary to get the results we want. When things are non-trivial but documentation is available, we won't pose a problem to others that need to work with our code. What if the lead programmer keeps most knowledge about the system in his or her head? Well, if you happen to employ this lead programmer, this involves a big risk to you: Your system is built around a single, irreplaceable person. If this person leaves your company or gets involved in a traffic accident, you're in trouble.

If you *are* this lead programmer, well done: You are irreplaceable and can ask for any salary you want. Not because of your competence but because of your lack thereof. If you get bored of the system that you're working on, tough luck. Nobody can take your place.

It is beneficial to both sides to have a properly documented system. Writing documentation is a task that nobody seems to enjoy. It may be worth it to outsource this task to a student, who will learn a lot from the experience. The following paragraphs deal with making the code itself more transparent, and reducing its learning curve.

8.1 No hard-coded, undocumented values

It takes a minimal effort to write code like the following, but reading and understanding it is definitely much more difficult.

```
switch (objectdatatype.ToLower())
{
    case "st":
        intML=255;
        break;
    case "si":
        intML=5;
        break;
    case "dt":
        intML=10;
        break;
    default:
        intML=0;
        break;
}
```

From a technical point of view, the above code is crystal clear. Few language constructs are as transparent as a `case` statement. What makes the code hard to understand is the fact that it is full of hard-coded, constant values that appear to have some meaning, but this meaning is not explained by the code. We can only guess what `si` means and why the magic number 10 is used in branch `dt`. When we define constants earlier on in the code and provide them with comments, a lot of guesswork can be prevented:

```
const DATATYPES_STRING="st"; // STring
const DATATYPES_NUMBER="si"; // Short Int
const DATATYPES_DATE="dt";   // DaTe

/* length of short strings is
   0..255 stored in 1 byte */
const MAXLEN_STRING=255;

/* max number=16 bit=65535
   =5 digits */
const MAXLEN_NUMBER=5;

/* yyyy-mm-dd=always 10 chars */
const MAXLEN_DATE=10;


switch (objectdatatype.ToLower())
{
    case DATATYPES_STRING:
        intML=MAXLEN_STRING;
        break;
    case DATATYPES_NUMBER:
        intML=MAXLEN_NUMBER;
        break;
    case DATATYPES_DATE:
        intML=MAXLEN_DATE;
        break;
    default:
        intML=0; // invalid type
        break;
}
```

Even with the slightly clumsy naming of variable intML in the code, at least it is a lot more understandable what the values mean. We should keep in mind that what may be crystal clear to us, may be an absolute mystery to others.

8.2 Name boolean functions by behaviour

In the case of boolean functions, we can make an agreement that their name should start with a second-person verb such as 'is', 'has', 'must', 'can' or other verb that will help indicate what result will be expected from the function in what situation. The following is a counter-example of a function prototype:

```
bool validatedata(DataObject data);
```

Will this function return TRUE or FALSE if the validation fails? By this interface definition, we can not read what value is returned in which situation. The return value TRUE could either mean "yes, the data was valid" or "yes, an error has occurred". When the function name starts with a verb (is, has, can, must) and is followed by a noun or adjective, or (even better) both, the return value of the function will automatically become much clearer:

- `bool isDataValid(DataObject data)`
  will probably return `true` if the data is valid

- `bool isDataInvalid(DataObject data)`
  will probably return `false` if the data valid

- `bool hasValidContent(DataObject data)`
  will probably return `true` if the content is valid

- `bool fileExists(string filename)`
  will probably return `true` if the file exists

8.3 Limit length and width of functions

Functions that span a multitude of pages are not acceptable. It shows that something is wrong with the level of detail of the function. Because of this, the readability of the function is reduced. By lack of other guidelines, you should make sure that functions should not exceed a page when printed in a normal font on a sheet of letter size paper (or A4 sized paper, if that is what you print on).

Rather than speaking of the width of functions, we might speak of the maximum line length used in functions. Bugs may hide and be overlooked in the hidden part of the line.

If a line of code does not fit on the screen horizontally, split it up. In case of variable screen size, a maximum of 80 characters is often recommended.

Rather than splitting up a line in the middle of a word, choose a logical place to split up the line – for instance between function arguments, after a comma or before an operator.

8.4 Write modular code

The time that it takes a programmer to get used to a system, depends on the amount of knowledge required to work on that system safely and effectively. To minimize the effort, it helps to design systems as blocks inside blocks inside blocks; Each of these blocks should only communicate with its direct neighbours, and affect only its own state and scope[19].

The other key to modular code is functional separation. Each part of the system, be it a procedure, a button on a user interface or even a variable, should perform exactly one function. This means, among other things, we should steer clear of functions that do everything, buttons with alternating labels and carelessly re-using variables for various purposes.

When a system is poorly designed, and various parts are entangled in each other, a much bigger part of the system must be understood before it can be modified without causing dependent code to break. The performance of the programmers working on the system is then only related to how familiar a programmer is with the given system. This can be a very frustrating experience, especially to skilled new team members who know very well how to write proper code.

In contrast, when a system has a proper modular design, little knowledge about the system is necessary to be able to start working on it in a safe and effective manner. As changes to a module only affect that module, new programmers will be able to become productive team members in a very short amount of time- sometimes from the first day on.

---

19 This is a simplified explanation of what is commonly known as the Law of Demeter.

8.5 Use a clear naming convention

When naming variables, functions or procedures, the chosen name should be sufficiently descriptive. The only exception to this rule are loop counters, where for decades single-letter variable names such as `i` have been used (originally to conserve memory).

Prevent abbreviations whenever possible, because the loss of information may cause fellow programmers to get confused about the meaning of the name. This will cost a lot more productivity than the seconds saved by using abbreviated names. In addition to the fact that most programmers can type fairly quickly, modern development environments have code completion, which will allow you to type long variable names as quickly as short ones. A benefit of using non-abbreviated variable names is that it will not only make clearer what a variable name means; it also clears the confusion such as "What was the name of that variable again, `passwd` or `password`?"

In many programming languages, variable names are case sensitive. That is, `variablea` and `VariableA` are two different variables. Do not choose variable names that can only be distinguished from each other by their case.

There is somewhat of a convention that variables written entirely in UPPERCASE refer to predefined constants or enumerations. As for variables, there are two popular conventions of variable naming: by using `MixedCase` variable naming, and by using `lowercase` variable naming. Each convention has their advantages. Naming variables in `lowercase` has the advantage that you will be able to port code from that platform to any other platform without need to change the existing convention, though this might not be an important consideration.

Some people argue that Mixed Case naming is more readable, because the case of the characters indicates where words start and end. Spelling mistakes caused by the wrong case are easy to make and hard to find by eye, however, and it may sometimes be unclear which characters to capitalize if a word could equally well be considered two words. Fortunately, our compilers can help us find spelling errors by only accepting pre-declared variable names.

The people that prefer working in lowercase often enhance readability of their variables by means of underscores, for instance by writing person_name rather than personname. It is as easy to accidentally end up with both variables personname and person_name as it is to accidentally end up with PersonName and Personname. The risk is equal, so one isn't better than the other.

Use any convention that suits you, just do not mix conventions in a single system. If a system already follows one convention, follow that convention.

To avoid confusion, prevent using different variable names that are spelled equally, such as person_name vs. personname, or in case you use a case sensitive language, variable names that can only be distinguished by their capitalization (such as Personname and PersonName).

In object-oriented programming, there may be some extra confusion between properties and parameters of a method. For instance, consider the code on the following page:

```
class Person
{
    private string name;
    Person::Person(string name)
    {
        this->name=name;
    }
}
```

In object-oriented programming, we may often allowed to omit the reference to the current object, `this->`. If accidentally we write `name` instead of `this->name`, our code won't do a thing, possibly without the compiler warning us. It's clear that we should distinguish between parameters and properties.

For this reason you may want to prefix either method properties or function parameters to make this distinction, or give them different names altogether. Either way helps prevent confusion. In the following example, the chance of variable names getting mixed up is virtually zero; if we write `this->person_name` or accidentally leave out the `this->` prefix before writing `name`, the compiler will raise an error.

```
class Person
{
    private string name;
    Person::Person(string person_name)
    {
        this->name=person_name;
    }
}
```

8.6 Avoid multiple declarations per line

Various languages allow us to declare multiple variables or arrays on a single line. In general, however, it is better to avoid this feature, as it can have side effects when not approached carefully.

In languages in the C family, we might carelessly write the following declaration:

```
char* a,b,c
```

This will declare only variable a as pointer to a char, whereas variables b and c are declared as char.

Languages in the Visual Basic family have a similar flaw:

```
Dim a,b,c As String
```

will declare only variable c as string, whereas the other variables, lacking an explicit type definition, are declared as variants.

By declaring only one variable per line, we avoid these ambiguities. As an added bonus, this gives us the space to write in-line documentation for the use of each variable, for instance:

```
char* tmpfilename; /* full path+name */
char* filekey;     /* filename only */
```

8.7 Parameterize all your error messages

Generating error messages by itself is simple enough. Consistently generating error messages that are useful and informative to whomever runs into them is harder. In most (if not all) cases, however, there is a considerable added value to adding a parameter in your error messages. This will significantly reduce the time that your fellow programmers need to find a bug. It may also give more advanced users a clue about what they can do to resolve the problem by themselves.

For example:

```
File not found
```

This may trigger our response: Which file was the system looking for?

```
File '<filename>' not found
```

A bit better. The quotes make sure that empty file names won't go undetected. So, we know what wasn't found, but we don't know where the system has been looking for it.

```
File '<filename>' not found
in search path '<path>'
```

Ah, that makes sense, at least to us programmers. Perhaps for users we want to hide this technical information in a details section of the error dialog.

Say, for instance, we just defined a database table with some 20 new columns, and run a big set of queries on that table. After a while we get an error message:

```
YSE-00A05: column name is invalid
```

If we're lucky, the message has something to do with the table we just added. If not, we're going to have to painfully browse through all possible queries that may have been issued to the database. In the best case, we need to check which of the 20 column names was misspelled.

An error message

```
Invalid column name:
 'pesron_name' in table 'person'
```

would have immediately cleared this up.

As you can see, adding one or more parameters to an error message will easily save our fellow programmers, our clients and ourselves a lot of trouble. This is one programming habit that you should pick up immediately if you haven't already.

8.8 Keep your code neatly layout

It is worth it to keep the layout of your code tidy. When talking about tidy code layout, I mean positioning of brackets, usage of white space, and proper indenting. This will help make your code easy to read. Unfortunately, there are different opinions about what is best,

Which of the following is better, the left hand side or the right hand side?

Compact layout	*Spaced layout*
```if (a==1) { do_something(); }```	```if (a==1) { do_something(); }```
```if (a==1) { do_something(); }```	```if (a == 1) { do_something(); }```
```if (a==1) { do_something(); }```	```if (a==1) { do_something(); }```

The left-size version has the benefit that code takes a bit less space. As such, more code can be displayed at once. The right-side version is a bit easier on the eyes.

The very thing that is considered a benefit in one point of view, is considered a drawback in the other. It just depends on what you consider to be more important.

Follow whatever convention seems to be in effect; it is not worth quarrelling about, and choosing one way over the other is not going to change the quality of your software.

No matter what layout you choose, if you can, perform code layout automatically rather than manually. Not only will this save time, but it will also help enforce a consistent layout between team members. If you work with Visual Studio, you will find that code layout tools are already available in your integrated development environment. In other cases, code may be automatically formatted by command line utilities for the language or languages that you work with.

8.9 Name for maximum readability

The general consensus seems to be that fixed-space fonts are more readable for program code than proportionally spaced fonts. However, some fixed-space fonts make it difficult to distinguish the upper-case letter O and the number 0, as well as the characters | (vertical line or pipe), I (capital i), l (lower-case L) and 1 (one).

When your variable names contain such characters, this will make some errors hard to spot, and when displayed in a certain font even impossible. Can you spot which character is what in the following code[20]?

```
variab0=0;
variab1=1;
```

To yourself, you can make things easier by choosing a font that clearly distinguishes between these similar looking characters.

---

20 Answer: variab zero equals upper-case O, variab one equals lower-case L.

8.10 Add useful comments to your code

Source code should contain enough comments to make clear what the code is doing, how, and why. A good habit that some programmers have is to write down their source as commented pseudo-code first, then to add real code in between - this will guarantee that the 'how' part is covered, although the programmer might forget to explain what the code is for.

Some programmers are of the opinion that the 'how' part should already be sufficiently explained by the code itself, and that writing it down as comments is a duplicate effort. Provided the code is readable enough, this is no problem:

```
// Bananas
Process_fruits("Bananas");

// Grapes
Process_fruits("Grapes");

// Apples
Process_fruits("Apples");
```

The comments in the above example have no added value whatsoever, because the code itself is already equally clear about what it is doing. In combination with the spacing, the comments makes the code take up three times the screen space that it needs to. The code is better off, and equally clear, with the comments and white space left out.

Some rules can be followed to make comments useful. Every function-definition should start with a comment that describes what the function is for, what parameters it accepts and what return value we can expect from the function, given certain input. Other useful places are in the separate branches of an IF statement, and in the beginning of a loop.

Possibly the most useful type of comment you can add are comments that double as documentation for the system. As the documentation is written along with the system, most likely the documentation will stay up to date better than when it would be written separately. Some tools exist that will allow you to generate documentation for your system based on the content of comments. Examples of such tools are Doxygen and JavaDoc. Tools of this sort generally assume that you have set up the comments in your system in a certain way. For instance, the comments that are to be included in the documentation start with with /** instead of /* or with three slashes instead of two. In other words, they are still syntactically valid comments in a normal context, but the documentation system will know that only these comments are intended to be added to the documentation.

In a system that is actively being developed, it can be useful to add little comment snippets that show who made a change to a piece of code. Of course you should already be able to figure this out by having version control operational, but when the comment itself contains this information, we can save ourselves the time needed for looking it up. A good example of a comment snippet is:

```
/* Bug 42 */
```

Even better is to write the snippet in the following manner (which will save our co-workers more time than it takes us to write it):

```
/* Bob - Bug 42, added precondition check
   for object3 */
```

This points us to bug number 42 in our bug tracking system and briefly describes what it is about. Writing a comment like this will cost just about no time at all, while the bug system can contain all additional information required to have a full understanding of what the code is about. We should be aware that dependence on the bug tracking system will cause the comments to no longer stand for themselves.

In some cases, we may use several bug tracking systems (for instance one at the client, one internally), in which case our comment snippets should somehow indicate in which bug tracking system the appropriate problem description can be found.

Finally, by popular convention, comments starting with `TODO:`, `FIXME:` or `BUG:` indicate that an action is required in the code near the comment. This allows the developer quickly search for unresolved issues in the code. Some development environments will use such comments to display a handy list of tasks yet to complete.

8.11 Avoid hidden errors

Most modern programming languages have some means of error-trapping, be it as `try/catch`, `ON ERROR`, `TRY/END TRY`, `eval/if ($@)` or similar construct. This is very useful to recover from severe errors that may occur for reasons beyond our control. Instead, error trapping mechanisms are often abused to hide sloppy programming from users- an anti-pattern known as *error hiding*. An example:

```
try
{
    x=document.getElementById("name").value;
    /* [block of mission critical, bug free
       code that we wrote] */
    alert(x);
}
catch (ex)
{
    /* empty catch block; errors in the
       entire try block are hidden */
}
```

When any runtime errors are present in the above `try` block (for instance because the `name` field does not exist), execution of the rest of the block is interrupted. Our mission critical code is not executed. Also, when new code is added to the `try` block, it will be difficult to properly test it, because no runtime errors will ever be visible, even if they occur. As a result, bugs may slip through. Worst of all, while the system *appears* to work correctly, unpredictable behaviour may occur, but only become visible when it is already too late. Without any error messages, it can be very hard for other programmers to trace where the actual mistake took place. In this case, the whole `try..catch` clause is nothing but a cover-up that makes life more difficult for other programmers.

Even if we do not want to show the users any errors that are the result of sloppy programming, empty `catch` blocks (or empty error handles in general) are simply not acceptable because invariably they will cause programmers to spend more time debugging and less time being productive. The very least we can do is to log errors behind the scenes- making sure that this logging itself can never trigger recursive exceptions, of course.

This small investment in time will earned back on the first occasion that an error is caught, because the log file will immediately inform us where a bug is hiding.

Apart from making sure that the error handling provides us with useful information, it is also highly recommended to make error traps span as few instructions as possible. This has a few benefits:

- It will make it easier to pinpoint the exact location where the error condition occurred

- It helps prevent us from accidentally hiding other errors

- It helps us not to disrupt the normal flow of the program, reducing the chances that unintentional behaviour occurs.

As a rule of the thumb, exception handling or error trapping should only be used for situations that are beyond our control. Our own code should obviously not fall into that category. Whenever our code catches an error, it should deal with the situation gracefully.

8.12 Be consistent

If various pieces of code are written by consistently following the same rules, it will be easier for another programmer to start working on a piece of code that (s)he has never seen yet, because the methodology in it will match the usual.

It is understood that consistency can be hard to enforce within large programming teams. In that case, the teams first need to agree on which conventions will be consistently followed. See if it is possible to enforce coding conventions automatically, rather than depending on discipline.

If it is not possible to enforce the coding conventions automatically, at least make sure that the conventions are well-documented and clear to all programmers on the team. Make sure that all programmers stick to the documented rules by making someone responsible for enforcing the coding conventions.

It is likely that enforcing coding conventions manually will require a considerable effort; this is why enforcing such conventions automatically is preferred.

Chapter 9

Optimizing your code

The first home computer that I had regular access to was pretty much top of the line when we got it. It ran at 3 MHz, had 16 kilobyte of RAM, an additional 16 kilobyte of video RAM (oh luxury!) and read programs from audio tape, recorded at a baud rate of 300 bit per second. As such, a one-hour tape would contain roughly 128 kilobytes of data.

Bill Gates is now ridiculed for saying "640 kilobytes ought to be enough for everyone"[21]. Not strange, considering the fact that computers nowadays are extremely powerful compared to the ones back then. Nowadays, we won't be surprised if we hear a computer runs at 3 gigahertz, has 1 gigabyte of RAM, 256 megabytes of video RAM and a 200 gigabyte hard drive[22].

---

21 He never actually said that.
22 Unless you read this text a few years after it was written, and only obsolete computers will have such poor specs.

To put this in perspective, compared with the computer I started with, nowadays a nice computer has at least 1000 times the clock speed, 65536 times the RAM, 16384 times the amount of Video RAM and over a million times the amount of storage. Speed for accessing that storage are immense: data rates of over 10 megabyte per second are pretty common. In addition, you may have a 2 megabit per second or better internet connection and a gigabit LAN.

We should, as such, face a reality. Computers nowadays are speed-monsters. With a machine that powerful, if your code is slow, you must have done something awfully wrong. Because of this, the most important rule about optimizing your code is: Do not optimize your code. Instead, write it in such a way that it will not need optimizing.

The following paragraphs will give tips and tricks that will help prevent the need for optimization. In addition, should you get to the point where you *do* need to optimize your code, the described techniques will be a good starting point.

9.1 If possible, do not optimize

The first rule in optimization is: don't optimize. However, there are situations in which system performance is so poor that something must be done to solve the problem.

Before you optimize, make sure that the optimization is desirable and worth it. Be aware that there may be some serious downsides to optimization. Optimizing may cost time and maintenance, and often sacrifices code clarity.

Premature optimization might prove to limit the flexibility of the system in a later stage. There is such a thing as things running fast enough; if you can get away with it, do not optimize.

It may be cheaper to get a heavier machine by the time your system gets too slow. It may be possible to archive old data to win back some speed. It may be possible that things are slow because the computer is swapping, in which case adding a bit of extra RAM will solve the problem. Of course, the possibility to throw more hardware at a problem is no excuse for badly written code, but sometimes it is the most cost-effective solution.

If you really can't escape optimizing your code, it is worth it to have your optimization strategy planned out. I hope the following paragraphs will be of assistance in this.

9.2 Perform trivial optimization

In optimizing code for optimal performance, the first thing we learn is to prevent unnecessary calculations and operations. It is literally the oldest trick in the book, but this text would not be complete without it, so here we go.

```
function uppercase(string strInput)
{
    string strOutput="";
    for (i=0;i<strlen(strInput);i++)
    {
        if ((substr(strInput,i,1)>="a")
        &&(substr(strInput,i,1)<="z"))
        {
            strOutput=strOutput+
            chr(
                asc(
                    substr(strInput,i,1)
                )-32
            );
        }
        else
        {
            strOutput=strOutput+
            substr(strInput,i,1);
        } /* end else */
    } /* end for */

    return strOutput;
}
```

The above function returns the upper-case version of an ASCII string. Calculating the length of a string (done by the function `strlen`) and getting a substring from a string (done by the function `substr`) may be heavy operations, yet they are performed repeatedly.

If we limit the amount of function calls by storing their result in a variable, our code will most likely be faster. In the above case, any loop iteration may be forced to recalculate the length of the string. In case of a 'zero-terminated' string, this may be a very heavy operation, growing heavier as the string grows longer. The reason for this is that the length calculation needs to scan the string for the terminator character, one character at a time. As such, figuring out the string length of a string N characters long will take N operations.

This is, of course, if the strings library of the programming language in question works as described. If it simply keeps track of the length of a string by storing it in a separate word in the string data structure, retrieving the string length can be done in constant time.

This shows a risk of optimizing: time is spent on improving code, but sometimes these improvements may be based on incorrect assumptions about the underlying system. To prevent building on incorrect assumptions, all we need to do is to call the string library functions with both short and long strings and measuring if the difference in performance is expected to be worth our effort.

For the case of this example, we'll assume that we found out that calculating the string length and extracting substrings are indeed slow operations. Now consider the following code.

```
function uppercase(string strInput)
{
    string strOutput="";
    int slength=strlen(strInput);
    for (i=0;i<slength;i++)
    {
        char currchar=substr(strInput,i,1);
        if ((currchar>="a")
        && (currchar<="z"))
        {
            strOutput+=
                chr(asc(currchar)-32);
        } else {
            strOutput+=currchar;
        } /* end else */
    } /* end for */
    return strOutput;
}
```

This piece of code will most likely run faster, because it only calculates the string length once: before entering the loop. This means that while looping, the calculation is not done over and over again. In addition, the substring containing the character being processed is also only extracted from the string once per iteration. Overall, this also improves maintainability and readability; the variable names end up being more descriptive than the code that they replace, and if the code needs to change, it will only be in one place. This means that even if the performance win is marginal, it would still be beneficial to write your code like this.

The good thing about this practice is that we can implement it as we write our code; it does not have to be done afterwards.

9.3 Be aware of the Big O

In information analysis, there are only 3 different numbers: zero, one and many. If you do not require processing any items, no room for optimization there. If you can avoid processing 1 item, great. However, optimization mostly deals with the latter case: 'Many'. If you need to sort 'many' items, how much time does it take? If you need to search for an item in a list of 'many' items, how much time does it take?

'Big O' notation is used to indicate the order of efficiency of an algorithm compared to the size of a given problem. We can attempt to measure and graph the performance of a system after we've built it, but often this is not necessary as the performance can be roughly predicted while we are writing the code. Although the following is not exact, it gives a pretty usable 'rule of the thumb' indication of the efficiency of certain programming techniques:

- The ideal case is when an algorithm runs in $O(1)$, it means it runs in a constant amount of execution time regardless of the size of the problem to solve. Hash algorithms generally fall into this category. Usually, the trade-off is more memory usage.

- If a piece of code runs in $O(n)$ time, it means that the execution time is proportional to the size of the problem. A single, unnested loop is a common example of this.

- If a piece of code runs in $O(n^2)$, it means that typically the execution time rises proportionally to the square of the size of the problem. This happens for instance when we nest a loop inside a loop. Algorithms of this order are not scalable. A common example is bubble sort. We should be aware that a function containing a loop called from within a loop in another function also runs in $O(n^2)$.

- Likewise, code running in $O(2^n)$ will not scale well. Encryption algorithms are deliberately designed in such a way that the only way of decrypting a message without the appropriate key is by trying all possible combinations. As such, cracking a message encrypted with a 128 bit key would require up to 2^{128} attempts.

- If a piece of code runs in $O(log(n))$, the algorithm gets more and more efficient as the size of the problem increases, because in each step of solving the problem, the size of the problem is reduced by a certain factor. As such, algorithms of this order are scalable too. A common example of this is a binary search tree.

Obviously, the algorithm that we choose to use greatly impacts the efficiency and scalability of our code. When writing a piece of code, we should consider both the average (expected) efficiency of the code and the worst-case efficiency.

9.4 Optimizing by memoization

Memoization is an optimizing technique similar to caching, which can be applied to referentially transparent functions (functions that always return the same output given the same input) that perform repetitive operations. For example, the following is a naive implementation of an algorithm that calculates the factorial of a number:

```
function fact(int x) returns int
{
    if (x<=1)
    {
        return 1;
    }
    return x*fact(x-1);
}
```

When we follow the program flow to look at how the result is calculated, we will find:

```
fact(1) =         1
fact(2) =       2*1
fact(3) =     3*2*1
fact(4) = 4*3*2*1
```

We see that as the value of n grows, the efficiency drops, while tail of the calculation is always repeated. We could try to cache the tail, by implementing the function slightly differently.

The following implementation assumes a programming language that features static variables, meaning variables that are remembered after exiting a function. If your language of choice does not feature static variables, you can simulate them by declaring them as private class member or even as global variables - as long as you make sure that they are used by *only one* function.

```
function fact(int x) returns int
{
    const MAXNUM=1000;       // cache size
    static int mem[MAXNUM]; // result cache

    /* The result cache must be initialized
       to contain only 0 values before use */

    if (x<=1)
    {
        return 1;
    }

    if (x>=MAXNUM)
    {
        // out of range for cache, so calculate
        return x*fact(x-1);
    }

    if (mem[x]!=0)
    {
        // result is already cached, return cache
        return mem[x];
    }

    // Not yet in cache,
    // calculate result and cache it
    mem[x]=x*fact(x-1);
    return mem[x];
}
```

In the above case, the original algorithm happened to be very short, but for larger pieces of code the absolute number of lines to add should stay about the same: three if statements and a static array to cache function results.

As you may have noticed, caching aside, the actual algorithm itself still functions pretty much as before and hasn't suffered all that much rewriting. The main difference is that it reuses a previous result, if possible, and otherwise stores the result of the current calculation for future lookup.

There is a slight bit of added complexity because the above example limits itself to remembering a maximum of 1000 numbers. In the above example, the code assumes that all array elements are automatically initialized to 0 before use. This is used to indicate whether an element is already cached or not.

The spectacular part about memoization is that it actually alters the order of the algorithm, with almost no rewriting work at all.

Where the original factorial ran in $O(n)$, the algorithm that uses cached results will run in constant time or $O(1)$. For larger values of n it will run in $O(n - \text{MAXNUM})$.

9.5 Prevent iterations and recursion

A loop is such an elementary construct in programming, that it is hard to imagine working without it. Yet, using loops inside loops inside loops inside loops will cause your system to get slower and slower, as the execution time of part of the program goes from $O(n)$ to $O(n1 * n2)$ to $O(n1 * n2 * n3)$.

One of the most frequently used operations is finding an item in a list. If you need to find an item in a list, you can simply start iterating the list until you find the item. If the list is sorted, you can start in the middle and do a binary search, which is already a lot more efficient.

If you have the RAM (nowadays rarely a problem), you can possibly prepare a hash table and simply check if for the existence of the element at the calculated position. Good news: most modern languages have a construct known as a HashTable or Associative Array, which allows looking up elements in a table by their name, rather than by a numeric index. Note the use of a separator to simulate a multi-dimensional associative array; this works well, but we have to make sure that normal keys do not contain this separator.

```
HashTable pricelist=new HashTable();
/* The following separator never occurs in
    prodtype/prodcolor: */
const string SEPARATOR="__";
string prodtype="toy car";
string prodcolor="red";
string prodsize="small";

pricelist.Add(prodtype+SEPARATOR+
              prodcolor+SEPARATOR+
              prodsize,(float)4.95);
```

In general, built-in associative arrays of a language such as in Perl and PHP, or standard data structures such as HashTables that are present in DotNet or Java are a lot more efficient than doing a search by ourselves, and save us the need to use a loop.

A real HashTable is one of the most efficient data structures that exists for purposes of looking up data. Writing data might be a bit more CPU-intensive.

Getting an item from the price list as defined in the example above could be as simple as:

```
float price=(float)pricelist.GetObject(
    "toy car"+SEPARATOR+
    "red"+SEPARATOR+
    "small"
);
```

This would calculate a single hash, and simply get the element from the hash table with that hash, most likely in $O(1)$ or $O(log(n))$, depending on the algorithm used to implement it.

The following naive equivalent without associative arrays would probably have been something along the following lines. Not only is the code itself more cluttered, but it will also execute far slower than the previous example.

```
string strDesiredprodtype="toy car";
string strDesiredprodcolor="red";
string strDesiredprodsize="small";
int prodtypeindex=0;
int prodcolorindex=0;
int prodsizeindex=0;
for (i=1;i<=TOT_PRODTYPES;i++)
{
    if (prodtype[i]==strDesiredprodtype)
    {
        prodtypeindex=i; break;
    }
}
for (i=1;i<=TOT_PRODCOLORS;i++)
{
    if (prodcolor[i]==strDesiredprodcolor)
    {
        prodcolorindex=i; break;
    }
}
for (i=1;i<=TOT_PRODSIZES;i++)
{
    if (prodsize[i]==strDesiredprodsize)
    {
        prodsizeindex=i; break;
    }
}
float price=pricelist[prodtypeindex]
            [prodcolorindex][prodsizeindex];
```

This could be optimized by using three binary trees, for example.

But before we lose ourselves in optimizing anything, let's take a look at the former example code again:

```
float price=(float)pricelist.GetObject(
    "toy car"+SEPARATOR+"red"+SEPARATOR+
    "small");
```

Obviously it will cost less time to write code like this than to optimize the existing code.

In addition, looking up items by an index will often cost fewer comparison operations than when a forest of if statements is used- especially when those if statements are used in a loop.

Now you see why I said before: Do not optimize your code. Instead, write it in such a way that it will not need optimizing.

9.6 Optimize only if there is a bottleneck

In general, when our code is too slow, there is a bottleneck. This can be in computations, but it can also be in the communication of the computer with its peripherals, be it the screen, printer, disk, network or others. Before you start optimizing, make sure there is a bottleneck, and figure out where it is.

Often, I/O operations are slow. We can boost their performance by caching. Once, I spent a day on writing a caching algorithm, only to find out that things ran slower after optimizing them - because, as it turned out, the system used all its free RAM as disk cache anyway. The existing cache worked better than the one I implemented. What went wrong was that I tried to eliminate a bottleneck that wasn't there. Because of this, we should measure which pieces of code use how much execution time.

Profiling tools can be a big help in finding the offending piece of code, although companies often do not supply such tools to their employees.

We can however perform some simple measurements without such specialized tools, by simply reading the timer before and after executing a piece of code to find out which piece of code is the offending one. If necessary, execute a piece of code several thousand times to get a more precise average runtime. This will also reveal the presence of a cache, in the case of I/O operations.

9.7 Prepare data to prevent bottlenecks

When optimizing our code, we replace slow code by faster code. For the best possible performance, often we have to make a trade-off; usually this trade-off is increased complexity or a larger memory footprint.

In some cases, we can pretty much predict what functions will be called by our code. For instance, before math co-processors were common, programs that would show graphical animations would calculate a sine/cosine table in advance, because doing a lookup was much faster than performing the actual calculation. The downside was that the table required some RAM, and of course the precision of the table was limited compared to the calculation.

In the past I built a system that displayed survey results on a website. In an early version, calculating the full set of data to display on the website would cost 20 minutes. As such, it was done periodically on the server, once per hour. This was an acceptable delay as the system was only fed with new data on a daily basis. However, by performing calculations in advance, the website was able to display any subset of the data to the end users almost instantly. The users were impressed with the performance, and the client was happy.

There was a reason for optimizing here, other than performance as perceived by the client. Each full system calculation took 20 minutes, making for a major delay in debugging and testing.

Also, the client had plans to take his company multi-national and wanted to run several sites on a single server. Just having three of them would have bogged down the server so much that it would constantly be calculating.

After redesigning and optimizing the calculation module, it took about 2 minutes to perform the full calculation. This was still too long to wait for when loading a web page, but a maximum delay of 5 minutes between entering data into the system and displaying it on the site was now possible.

Another popular use of the data preparation technique is to make web-based systems operate blazingly fast. A news website (typically non-interactive but featuring content management) may be written in PHP. If such a system generates the HTML for its pages every time the website content is altered, rather than on each incoming HTTP request, this will eliminate the need to interpret a slow script on each request.

The web server will simply be able to serve up the raw HTML pages, which is about the most trivial operation that a web server can handle. When all web pages are prepared and the entire site can be fully cached in RAM, such a server should be able to satiate a 100 Mbps link without breaking a sweat.

9.8 Spread out peak load

Often the reason that a program feels sluggish is because it attempts to do everything at once, creating a bottleneck in CPU power, network bandwidth or other resources. Often, the operations that need to be performed could be spread out over a larger period of time. The average load will remain about the same, but the peak load is greatly reduced, which can help creating a system that is much more responsive.

A computer is a machine that spends most of its time doing nothing at great speed. This idle time could be used in the background to do all kinds of useful operations. In the past, I wrote a training program that would decode its data files during idle time. When the user needed that data, it was usually already available. As a result, the program seemed extremely fast. In reality it just made efficient use of idle time. While users were reading through the course material that was presented by the program, the program was already busy decoding the next pages.

If spreading the load is not an option, we can make our users more tolerant to the wait by distracting them. This does not help response times and is more of a psychological optimization than anything else. Still, the users will tolerate, and might even enjoy being presented with a proper distraction. Splash screens or dialogs presenting a tip of the day can be nice ways to distract the user, and are a great time to prepare some data while the user is busy reading. A variation on this theme is displaying the user interface and playing make-believe that the system is ready for input, while in reality a lot of initialization is still going on. The user will be able to move around the mouse cursor and click, but the system will only be fully usable when it has completely initialized.

9.9 Prevent active waiting

Keeping the user entertained might be good on occasion, but if it happens too frequently it is not the answer. In a timesheet system that I once built, the finance department needed to actively wait for about a minute between confirmation operations. As it turned out, there was no way to perform the operations any quicker due to the limitations of the platform. As a result, it took over an hour lost in active waiting just to confirm the data entered by over 60 employees. Needless to say, the finance department was not amused.

The problem was solved by turning the time consuming task into a background task. Instead of actively waiting for the records to be confirmed, they were now merely set 'marked for confirmation' on the client side, which cost less than a second. A background agent on the server would detect which records were marked for confirmation and would periodically mark those records 'confirmed'. The total amount of time that it took to confirm the records was still equal- over an hour. But as this hour didn't require an manual action every minute, this hour could now be spent in a more productive manner.

Later on, at another employer, I found myself in a similar situation. The open source package PHProjekt required multiple slow submit actions to enter time sheet data of the various projects. Each and every project entered required reloading a web page various times. This web page was being run off-site and dreadfully slow. I built another, PHProjekt-compatible web interface, which limited submit actions as much as possible by usage of JavaScript and by showing a month worth of project data on a single screen.

After loading the initial page and showing 'ready', the rather long project list of the user was loaded in the background (in a hidden frame) in a few seconds, usually before the user could get to the point of clicking the 'choose project' button.

This button would run a Javascript which would instantly pop up this long list, sortable in various ways. This gave an extra feel of smoothness to the whole. After this new interface was done, I sent out an email saying "Feel free to try this alternative interface, feel free to stick to the original". After a few weeks, most of my co-workers had switched to the alternative interface, including the head of the department, who of course took credit for the idea.

One way to prevent active waiting is by turning a single-threaded application into a multi-threaded one. Effectively this means that some of the processing of the application is done as background process while the rest of the application continues responding to user requests.

There is a risk associated with this: debugging multi-threaded applications is considerably harder than debugging single-threaded ones. It is a must to read up on concurrent programming before going this way.

9.10 Allow a bit of quality loss

One way to achieve guaranteed fast response times is by reducing the quality of the result offered when the system is being stressed to its limits. These limits can be bottlenecks in any place: I/O throughput, network bandwidth, processor power, and so on. Examples are all around us:

- A text editor may interrupt rendering the current page when it detects that the page-down key is being pressed. As a result it will never fall behind and instantly render the correct page when the key is released;

- The sound quality of our cell phones will reduce when less bandwidth is available, but the latency between sender and receiver will remain constant;

- A web server may interrupt serving a page when the user has just requested another one.

- When fast-forwarding our CD player, it will not suddenly read audio blocks from CD at twice the speed. Instead, it may skip every other block. While burning a CD, skipping blocks is not an option. In such cases, features such as fast forward and rewind are disabled.

By determining which concessions we can make in the quality of the response, we can create systems that are a lot more responsive. In most cases, it will have been the user who was triggered the action that caused the quality loss, and there will be no need to make up for it.

9.11 Rewrite loops

In handling loops, a considerable amount of processor power is spent in checking if the loop is finished yet. The following code does this 1000 times:

```
int buffer=array();
for (int i=0;i<1000;i++)
{
        buffer[i]=0;
}
```

This overhead can be reduced by unrolling the loop; we simply place more code inside the loop and reduce the amount of iterations.

```
int buffer=array();
for (int i=0;i<1000;i+=4)
{
        buffer[i]=0;
        buffer[i+1]=0;
        buffer[i+2]=0;
        buffer[i+3]=0;
}
```

As the loop now only needs to be iterated 250 times to obtain the same result, the overhead that is added to the code by the loop is reduced considerably.

A drawback is that unrolling loops introduces some degree of code duplication. Also, compilers are often already capable of unrolling loops, so the performance gain may be marginal.

A bigger performance win can be expected if we simply employ a cleverer algorithm whenever possible. For instance,

```
int sum=0;
for (int i=0;i<1000;i++)
{
        sum=sum+i;
}
```

We can pair the values added to the sum as follows:

i=0 and i=999
i=1 and i=998
i=2 and i=997
    ...
i=n and i=999-n

As we pair the numbers, we can do with half the iterations, so we might as well rewrite the loop as follows:

```
int sum=0;
for (int i=0;i<500;i++)
{
        sum=sum+999;
}
```

Obviously, 500 times adding 999 to a sum is the same as a multiplication, so we can get rid of the loop altogether:

```
int sum=999*500;
```

By removing the loop altogether, the order of the loop has changed from $O(n)$ to $O(1)$, which will perform considerably better than the loop.

9.12 Optimizing interpreted code

Code that is interpreted, rather than compiled, will benefit to some degree from cutting out unnecessary weight. Interpreted code will run faster when short variable names are used rather than long ones, and when comments are removed.

It is important to realize that from a readability perspective, this is a terrible idea. Also, depending on the language, code that seems interpreted might actually be compiled on-the-fly or passed through a just-in-time compiler, making the benefit marginal. Your mileage may vary.

A similar argument applies to optimizing scripts that are downloaded on demand. If the bottleneck is the available bandwidth, it is likely that a lot more can be gained by compressing and decompressing the script on-the-fly, than by shortening variable names and leaving out comments.

This page intentionally left blank

Chapter 10

Tools

In designing and implementing systems, we do not live in an ideal world. Some tools that would be ideal to do a certain job may be too expensive to your employer due to licensing costs. This should however not be what decides the success of your project. When we put the tools that are available to their best possible use, the outcome will be the same.

10.1 Select the right tool for the job

Whenever possible, we should use the right tool for the job. If we need a system that provides reliable real-time information several times per second, a garbage-collecting language like Java probably isn't suitable, a language like C is probably more appropriate.

If we need a menu system that works on mobile phones and several operating systems, and real time operation is no issue, perhaps Java is a better choice than C.

Whoever wrote Tetris as an Excel spread sheet didn't do so because Excel was the right tool for the job, but to prove it could be done. If you are that person, I salute you; your project has great hack value. Don't do this in the boss' time.

To be able to make an informed decision about which tool to use for a particular purpose, it is necessary to get familiar with several of them. This is true for both programming languages and for supporting tools, such as bug tracking systems.

On the other hand, the ideal tool may be prohibitively expensive. If another tool isn't specifically intended for a given job, but it serves the purpose well, why not use it? Who hasn't ever hammered in a nail with something else than a hammer? Using the wrong tool often is better than using nothing at all. Of course, if you're stuck with writing to-do lists on paper, you may want to inform management that there is a better way.

10.2 Use the Internet

It has happened to me on many, many occasions that people requested my help to solve a problem they were having. Typically they would be confronted with some error message that they didn't understand.

Often such problem could be solved in a very short time by a combination of experience, intuition, and most of all by simply looking up the text of a received error message on the internet.

Especially Usenet (online at `http://groups.google.com`) is an extremely useful troubleshooting resource. Almost always there's someone that has faced the same problem before, and the solution is found quickly.

When it comes to actually finding tools, the internet is also the first place to search. There is a wealth of free development tools available. If commercial tools are too expensive, searching the web will generally offer an alternative, free solution.

As it turns out, support on open source software is pretty good. Especially if the software is backed up by an active community, mailing lists or forums can be a big source of help. When neither is available, proceed with caution. Authors of open source software are often very willing to help when you send them an email, but understandably don't like it when you waste their time with trivial issues. Most of them will however reply you, once, when you email them. They don't owe you anything, so use this one chance wisely. Keep your email short, polite and only resort to emailing the author directly if you have not found a solution otherwise.

10.3 Use Version Control

Implementing some type of version control is vital when a project is performed by multiple team members. The various version control systems make sure that the changes made by multiple people are well managed.

To do this, some version control systems block access to a file while it is being edited by a team member. Team members can work on a system simultaneously, as long as they only work in files not being used by others at the same moment. This leaves no doubt as to which version of a piece of code is the 'real' one, but files may be blocked more and more frequently as teams grow. One way to resolve this is to keep source files small; this makes it less likely that a file is needed by two people at the same time.

Other version control systems allow changes by multiple people at once. As long as the changes made by two or more people do not overlap, the changes can be merged without causing version conflicts.

Version control systems typically keep a full history of the changes made on a central server. In effect, this automatically documents which changes where made when by whom. All this is accomplished with a minimum of extra effort: Files are checked out before editing them (sometimes before each edit, sometimes only once, depending on the version control system), changes are made, and the changes are checked in again or committed. This implies there are multiple copies of each file: on both the version control server and the workstations of all developers involved. As a result, projects that employ version control rarely lose a lot of data, even if disaster strikes.

Both source code and documentation may be stored in version control systems, as both may be subject to frequent updates.

Even single developers may still benefit from using version control. You will be able to see which changes have been implemented when, and you will be able to easily revert to previous versions. Also, when working from different locations, or if you have written a library that you use in several projects, version control makes it easier to keep track which files represent the latest 'official' version of your system.

In a professional environment, a version control system is typically implemented on a server somewhere on the network. This will help ensure that work is not only stored locally on a workstation (which may be switched off at night), but on a server that is always available. It is also good idea to have the checked out files (or working directory) reside on a network share[23], so that they can be included in daily backups. This will help ensure that backups of all the latest work are made. Committed changes allow creating a 'nightly build' of the software by compiling and installing the latest version automatically each night, which in turn can be used for a regression test.

When choosing a version control system, an important consideration is the platform or platforms from which it needs to be accessed. If you work with exclusively with Visual Studio, using Visual Source Safe is the obvious choice. However, if you work in a multi-platform or UNIX-like setting, it makes more sense to choose CVS, Subversion (svn) or Trac. These will also work on Windows, and free client software can be found easily with your favourite search engine.

---

23 It would be recommendable that this network share resides on a different drive than the version control server uses for storage. This will help recovery in case of a drive crash.

10.4 Bug tracking/workflow

Bug tracking systems such as Bugzilla or Mantis are very useful to register bugs, but they have more uses. They are ideal to track the progress of solving bugs or implementing feature requests, but can also help project management. If a project is entered as a series of tasks with sufficiently small impact, the bug tracking system will very precisely show the progress of implementing new functionality.

More often than not, users of your system will also enter feature requests in the bug tracking system. This is where the availability of functional documentation starts to pay off. When the user can say "according to chapter 2, paragraph 3 of the documentation the system should behave like this or that", or if we can say "what you are asking conflicts with page x of the documentation", we save ourselves a lot of fruitless discussion with the client as of what should be part of the system and what should not.

A bug tracking system will serve to remind you which tasks are still to be done. give you structure in your work, and help you focus.

Whichever bug tracking system is decided on, it is important that using it is a minimal effort. If it is too much of a hassle to use a bug tracking system, it is likely that its users will at some point neglect to register small and seemingly unimportant issues in it. As proper procedures are not followed for these issues, this may ultimately result in increased maintenance costs.

10.5 Create a build server

It is extremely useful to have one or more machines dedicated to periodically occurring processes such as building your software[24] and creating backups. You will find these a worthwhile addition to your programming infrastructure. If several physical machines are not an option, consider virtual servers.

A build server may limit itself to pulling the last version of the software from the version control system and compiling it, but such a server can do much more for you: It can scan your software for common errors, package your software, forward it to the test server, publish it on a website for beta testing- the possibilities are endless.

A properly configured build server will save you a lot of work (mostly boring, repetitive jobs) and help you detect possible problems in an early stage, often within 24 hours from their occurrence.

In the best case, your build server will provide you with a one-step build process, so that building and packaging the software is trivial, even if there is little or no documentation.

---

24 Joel Spolsky has written the excellent article about this, "Daily Builds Are Your Friend" on his weblog: http://www.joelonsoftware.com.

10.6 Create a knowledge base

Knowledge should not be only in the head of the developers, it should be shared amongst them. This will help ensure the continuity of a project, when a developer gets ill or leaves the project for whatever reason.

To set up a knowledge base, a wiki seems a natural choice: It costs little effort to set up, makes it easy for everyone to contribute and share their knowledge, and the information will be easy to find back. A separate server to host the knowledge base is a good idea; not a lot of processing power is required, but it is important that plenty of disk space is available.

If high availability is not a requirement, a knowledge base may be run on cheap hardware, as long as backups are made on a regular basis.

Version control systems and wiki may compete over being the most suitable place to store knowledge. However, in general a wiki is easier to search and edit. If you set up a wiki, communicate this fact with the people that will use it. It may take a bit of time for the knowledge base to gain popularity, but as more and more questions are answered by it, it will be consulted more and more frequently.

New employees may well be the most suitable people to write 'getting started' style documentation, both because they're not tied up in projects yet, and because they will run into all the questions that are considered common knowledge by programmers that are already familiar with the system being developed. The effort will pay back for itself with every new employee being hired.

10.7 Set up your development environment

To work effectively, you will need to set up your development environment to allow you to be as effective as possible. This includes proper tools for writing documentation, programming, debugging, editing, quality control, any graphical work that you may need to do, and so on.

Make a list of software that you use; probably your co-workers have a set of favourites that they use on a daily basis, which may be worth investigating. You may have a few favourites yourself that you may share with others.

Perhaps your company enforces a policy about which software is acceptable and which software is not. In any case, you should be familiar with the choices that you have and use them to your best advantage. If certain tools are obviously missing from the list of acceptable software, you may have a say and have it added. Management usually has little trouble accepting productivity-boosting software that is free, legal and safe.

10.8 Use code analysis tools

There are some tools which analyze code to detect common problems in the code base. Code analyzers are generally relatively heavy-weight programs, and as such it may not be possible to perform a code analysis every time you compile your project. However, it may be a good idea to include such code analysis tools in the nightly build cycle to catch problems in an early stage. A few examples:

- Simian is a similarity analyzer. Its purpose is to detect duplicated code. Duplicated code is often a sign of copy/ paste programming, and it will lead to increased maintenance. By running a copy/paste detector in the build cycle, this increased maintenance can be prevented.

- Valgrind is a code analyzer for Linux that was originally intended to detect memory leaks, but nowadays it also has profiling capabilities.

Of course, if neither you nor your co-workers ever copy/paste code, a copy/paste detector is of little added value. Likewise, one doesn't necessarily *need* a memory leak detector to detect memory leaks. Writing wrapper functions for `malloc` and `free` to log memory usage can be just as effective, but the problem is to enforce this practice.

Including a few tools in the automated build cycle may prove to be less effort, and it will help the entire team to adhere to the same quality standards.

10.9 Create a toolbox

Whenever you find yourself repeating a chain of tasks or writing the same type of code over and over again, it is likely that you can save time by writing library functions and scripts to automate your tasks.

At some point, you will have a collection of scripts and library code that make your life a lot simpler. When sufficiently documented, your co-workers might benefit from this toolbox as well. Especially then, a small investment in time can have a big impact on overall efficiency.

Efficiency may be the main reason to start on a toolbox, but there are more reasons that are just as important.

- **Makes your work more interesting:** Manually repeating the same tasks over and over again is not only inefficient, it also makes your work more boring. Creating tools to solve such problems is a lot more fun.

- **Continuity**: If the build-and-release process within your company is a complex, multiple step operation, releasing a new version of a piece of software may be a daunting task, even if it is a thoroughly documented procedure. If the person responsible for releases is absent for whatever reason, the company may not be able to perform a software release. If, on the other hand, performing a software release is a one-click process, the software can be released at any given moment by anyone. If you must have a complex release procedure, creating a release wizard may solve your problem.

- **Quality**: By automating tasks that otherwise would require strong discipline, a higher quality standard can be reached. This can range from something as simple as automated reminders, to something as complex as enforcing strict coding standards.

Chapter 11

Prevent duplicate efforts

There are several ways of making sure that software stays maintainable. One of them is to make sure that when something needs to be changed, it needs to be done only once.

Not only will this be less work, which of course is nice, it will also help prevent the system to contradict itself, which makes it much easier to track down and fix bugs.

This chapter is dedicated to the rightfully lazy. It will give tips that allow us to do things in such a way, that we will need the minimum amount of effort to keep our system in the best possible shape.

11.1 Avoid copy/paste programming

In copy/paste programming, a snippet of code is duplicated several times in a project. Every time a bug needs to be fixed in a previously copied piece of code, or if something else needs changing in it, the change will need to be carried out in each individual clone of that code.

The problem is to track down all copies of the code. As the various copies of the code evolve in different ways, they become less and less similar to one another. This will make it more and more difficult to track down all copies of the code. The result is that problems that we thought we resolved, may reappear until finally we've fixed every broken instance of the code.

There is a better way: When instead we abstract the given piece of code into a function, we won't be confronted with this problem. A problem shows up, we track it down, we fix it on one place, and it is solved.

To help reduce maintenance, we can refactor pieces of code that are similar (but not equal) to contain the smallest amount of similarity possible. Using an array or hash table can help turning conditional behaviour into unconditional behaviour.

Consider the following example:

```
for (i=0; i<100; i++)
{
        if ((i mod 2)==0)
        {
                print "Number "+i+" is even";
                print "and that's how I like it";
                print "because even is the best!";
        }
        else
        {
                print "Number "+i+" is odd";
                print "and that's how I like it";
                print "because odd is the best!";
        }
}
```

We can reduce maintenance in this code by using an array to remove the conditionality of the code.

```
label[0]="even";
label[1]="odd";

for (i=0; i<100; i++)
{
        evenodd=label[i mod 2];
        print "Number "+i+" is "+evenodd;
        print "and that's how I like it";
        print "because "+evenodd+" is the best!";
}
```

The resulting code is not only shorter, it also needs to perform fewer comparisons than the original code. As a result, in addition to saving us maintenance, the resulting code will probably perform better.

When a `switch/case` statement is used instead of an `if`, this effect is amplified. There are legitimate uses for embedding a `switch/case` statement inside a for loop, but often it is an indication that the code is sub-optimal[25], both in maintenance and performance.

To help detect copy/paste programming in existing code, a similarity analyzer such as Simian can be helpful, but it is better to prevent code duplication altogether; As mentioned before, duplicates in code tend to become less and less similar as the system evolves.

When refactoring code, this best practice will most likely reduce the total number of lines in your code. This means that if management measures your productivity in lines of code per day, your productivity will seem negative. Make management aware of the fact that 'lines of code per day' is a very poor way to measure productivity. Generally, as programmers evolve their skills, they will need to write less and less code to solve a problem.

---

25 Indications that code is sub-optimal are also known as a 'code smells'. See 'The Pragmatic Programmer' by Andrew Hunt and David Thomas, Published by Addison-Wesley, Oct 1999 ISBN: 020161622X

11.2 Standardize validations based on type

When designing an input form, certain types of input validations can be generalized. For instance, in a consistent system, all date fields will allow the same characters, share the same date format, and so on. The same goes for number fields, for instance. This type of validation can be fully automated in a class (or derivative of an existing class).

As it turns out, we can distinguish several different types of validations.

- **Generic validations** that are strongly associated with the data type of a field. The term 'data type' in this context is to be seen in its broadest sense: A key field (regardless of it being a number or a string) is obligatory and its value must be unique; an integer field can contain only digits, a name field most likely will not contain numbers and be relatively short, whereas a description field can contain all kinds of textual nonsense. We can go a bit further than just considering something to be a 'text field': We can think of email fields, (web page)link fields, phone number fields, and so on. Once we develop a single generic piece of code to validate a certain field type, we can use that piece of code over and over again. Once we've written a generic validation for a certain data type, we won't ever need to write a single line of code again to perform that type of validation.

- The next type of validation can be implemented in a data driven manner and has to do with **range and precision**. When a person comes to the bank to open an account, his date of birth should be in the past, not in the future (unless the person is a time traveller). Any monetary amount first deposited most likely is positive, and probably has at most 2 decimals after the decimal separator. As you see, with this type of validation, we walk away slightly from the generic, because we are already in the realms of configuring the validations- but writing code is still not necessarily required.

- The last type of validation are completely **custom validations**, specific to a certain field. For instance, a date field containing birth date would normally have to fall a considerable amount before the wedding date of the same person. Or, if the user chooses option X in field Y, the value of the current field is not allowed to surpass the value 100. Most likely, these validations are too specific to be made configurable, and should simply be coded.

Writing code for generalized validations can often save a lot of time in correctly performing the validations themselves. In addition, the list of properties that can be configured for validating a data type can act as a check-list in communicating requirements with the client.

11.3 Save time with existing building blocks

If you need a function that is of average complexity, chances are that someone somewhere has already written that function. For example, if you need to check if something is a valid date, a function to check this is bound to already exist.

If you're working at a company and starting to implement a common functionality such as a user list, stop right there. First check if you can possibly import this data from an existing system.

Other than for educational purposes[26], there is no point in re-inventing the wheel over and over again by infinitely rewriting trivial functionality. If you find an existing function on the web, you're set- but it's even better to see if the framework that you're using or the environment in which you're working already contains a suitable alternative. In fact, it is your job to know the framework that you're using.

If we take in consideration that at big shot companies like IBM only 11 lines of debugged, documented code are written per programmer per day, this means that spending an hour of finding 10 lines of documented, debugged code will save you 7 hours of work. Keep in mind that 'lines of code per day' is a poor way to measure productivity, as good code is typically more compact than bad code.

---

26 From an educational perspective, it can be highly rewarding to create your own solution to existing problems. Be forewarned that from a problem-solving perspective, it is generally quite unproductive. However, if you have the time, designing your own networking stack or DBMS will most likely take you along the same paths as the masters before you, and it will give you a profound understanding of their inner workings.

It can be highly rewarding to be a bit creative in finding existing solutions to a problem. I remember implementing a string stack, after which a co-worker asked me why I would want to do that. He correctly pointed out that a string-list class was available, which could be used for the same purpose.

This shows that asking around can be a highly effective way of searching. If I would simply have asked "Does anyone have a string stack class?" I could have saved myself a few hours of work. On the other hand, my implementation performed significantly better than his, so the effort wasn't entirely wasted.

Of course, if you're too shy or too proud to ask your co-workers, your favourite search engine and/or Usenet will work magic too.

It should be noted that there are some risks involved in using existing building blocks, as in using any existing software. There may be licensing issues that need tending to.

Also, should there be bugs in those building blocks, we may not be able to fix them. This is not necessarily a problem; sometimes we can program around any bugs or limitations of a building block. Likewise, if there is a bug in the compiler that you use, often it is possible to work around it by writing down your code differently.

However, in writing safety-critical applications, using existing building blocks may simply not be good enough, just as much as using a consumer-level operating system may not be good enough for safety-critical systems. Only having the source code of a building block can guarantee whether it meets our quality standards.

11.4 Make it data driven

In making systems maintenance-free, an effective method is to move out things from the world of written code into the data domain. This allows us to store some aspects of the application as configuration in a database or configuration file, rather than having them hard-coded into the program.

To the client the benefit is that they have a bit more power over their application, allowing them to configure some of the inner workings of the system without need to constantly call upon the developer. To developers, there are considerable advantages as well:

- Fewer requests for trivial maintenance tasks, allowing us to focus on 'real' work.

- Data driven solutions tend to help prevent the temptation of copy/paste programming by centralizing values to a configuration file or database, which helps reduce duplicate efforts.

- A data driven application doesn't always need to be restarted after an update to the configuration, whereas if the same configuration were code driven, a system restart might be inevitable (unless the system is written in an interpreted language). This means that the availability of data driven systems is easier to guarantee than that of code-driven systems.

- In some cases, a data driven solution forces us to write out all possible scenarios that can take place, which guarantees that no cases are forgotten.

Code that uses values that are specified in configuration files nees to validate those values before use. This means that for correctness of the parameters, having a configuration tool available is not mandatory. If data changes frequently, providing our users with a configuration tool is probably a good idea.

We can go very far in making a system data-driven: It is possible to implement an entire system as a database-based solution, code and all- although in most cases this is a bad idea. As a rule of the thumb, things that change on a regular basis are good candidates for a data driven approach. Examples are access control lists, currency exchange rates and interest rates. Work-flow applications can be great candidates for a data driven approach as well, as business processes are subject to change all the time. A data driven solution may allow our customers to adapt the system to their business process, whereas a compiled, code driven solution certainly won't.

Rather than blindly deciding to turn the entire system into a data driven equivalent, we should first consider a few things:

- Is it beneficial to make it data driven?

- How often would changes be needed in a code-driven situation?

- How much time does it cost to turn it into a data driven situation?

- Is sufficient funding available?

- Will new code be written, or is refactoring needed? If code is being refactored, it is a good idea to write a unit test that will guarantee that the data driven version of the code behaves functionally identical to the original.

- Who will be maintaining the data driven configuration?

- How much time does it cost to train the client to use the data driven version of the solution?

- Is it realistic to assume the maintenance will be done by manually editing a text file or database table, or is a tool required?

- What is the impact on performance of the system?

11.5 Write knowledge-free functions

When functions contain the least amount of information about the environment in which they are operating, chances that they can be reused greatly increase. This is based on the *Principle of Least Knowledge.* Consider the following code:

```
bool isPersonTooOld(object person)
{
    // precondition checks left out to save space
    DateTime birth=person.birthdate;
    int age = DateTime.Now.Year - birth.Year;

    if (DateTime.Now.Month<birth.Month)
    {
        /* birthday this year is still to come */
        age--;
    }
    else
    {
        if (DateTime.Now.Month==birth.Month)
        {
            if (DateTime.Now.Day<birth.Day)
            {
                /* birthday is still to come */
                age--;
            }
        }
    }
    if (age>=65)
    {
        // person too old
        return true;
    }
    return false; // not too old
}
```

Altogether this function looks quite clean. Its reusability however is very limited, be it in other systems or even within the system itself.

This is caused by the function having specific knowledge of the system[27]: in this case the maximum allowed age of a person and the data structure of the person object. As a result, the following problems occur:

- The function can only check against a certain age. It would be better to add a parameter for age.

- Only applications that use a compatible person class will be able to use the function. It would be better to use a more generic data type such as DateTime.

Even if we apply the changes suggested above, we must take into consideration what the function call will look like, which will be something like

```
if (isPersonTooOld(person.birthdate,65))
{
    // person too old
}
```

As we can see, the function call does not explain if the age limit should be read as "65 years, inclusive" or as "65 years, exclusive".

---

27 Attentive readers will recognize that using global variables causes the same code reuse issue. Functions that contain global variables make assumptions about the environment that they live in.

A simple and elegant solution is to instead write a knowledge-free function. Because it doesn't try to tell any system what to look like, it is more easily accepted into any system. The following example shows what the code may look like:

```
int CalculateAgeInYears(DateTime agedate)
{
    int age = DateTime.Now.Year - agedate.Year;
    if (DateTime.Now.Month < agedate.Month)
    {
        return age-1;
    }
    if (DateTime.Now.Month == agedate.Month)
    {
        if (DateTime.Now.Day < agedate.Day)
        {
            return age-1;
        }
    }
    return age;
}
```

The associated function call is also more explicit about the behaviour of the system:

```
const MAXIMUM_AGE=65; // or get from database
int age=CalculateAgeInYears(person.birthdate);
if (age>=MAXIMUM_AGE)
{
    // person has reached age limit
}
```

This code explicitly shows that 65 years is already too old. As we can also see, the total amount of code has actually reduced, which will translate into lower maintenance, even if we use the function only once.

If necessary, we can maintain full compatibility with the old situation by creating a (hopefully temporary) wrapper function that will use the new function:

```
bool isPersonTooOld(object person)
{
    int age=CalculateAgeInYears(person.birthdate);
    if (age>=65)
    {
        return true;
    }
    return false;
}
```

We should be aware that while this allows us to maintain compatibility with an existing system, this is not ideal, as we will re-introduce a piece of code that is not reusable. If you can, avoid writing this wrapper function, or even remove the function isPersonTooOld altogether.

When the rewritten wrapper function is absent, your compiler will raise errors about this. This is a situation where the compiler actually works for us; by replacing these errors with the new, more explicit, reusable function call, we will be able to guarantee that no instance of the old function call remains in our code. Once our code compiles again, our code base will contain a bit more reusable code, making our work a bit easier than before.

For clarity, the above examples lack precondition checking. Rewriting the functions to include these checks is left as an exercise to the reader.

This page intentionally left blank

Chapter 12

Software Quality

The most often heard excuse for sloppy code and badly designed systems is time pressure. It costs time and money to deliver quality systems; time that is considered to be overhead, rather than part of the development process. It is a good thing that certain software companies are not in civil construction, or London Bridge would be falling down - several times a day.

It is true that building quality software costs time. Time to train people, to set up procedures, to test the written code, to document the system, and so on. But this is an investment that should pay back for itself after some time. After all, bugs that never happen cost less time and money to fix than bugs that have managed to cause severe damage.

Implementing a quality control system is about making sure that things will work properly, instead of hoping for the best. Ideally, this is done by making it as difficult as possible to make mistakes.

If we're placed in an environment that makes it impossible for us to make mistakes, we won't. But that won't necessarily make us productive. If we're being tied up, we won't get any work done. Creating a *productive* environment in which we cannot make mistakes is much harder - a continuous effort is needed to get to a point where mistakes are effectively prevented, but it can be done.

Each time a mistake is found, we should ask ourselves how we could have prevented that mistake, preferably in an automated manner. We should then implement a mechanism that will perform that automated mistake prevention. We, human beings, are simply too fallible to rely on.

12.1 Do not count on discipline

Managing programmers is commonly compared to herding cats. You can tell a cat not to touch the fish, but as soon as you're away, it'll do as it pleases. At the moment you're looking, it probably won't be anywhere near the fish, but as it is licking its paws it will give itself away. It would be foolish to tell a cat "I thought we agreed that you were going to stay away from the fish", because that won't solve the problem. The problem here is that it is not realistic to depend on discipline alone. Instead, put the fish out of reach of the cat and the problem will be solved.

Likewise, introducing countless rules for programmers to obey is just not going to work- At some point, there will be too many rules to remember. Under pressure, it will be too tempting to deviate from the rules. Discipline alone is obviously not enough to guarantee the quality of a system.

We can only prevent things from going wrong if we enforce discipline automatically, and if we have backup mechanisms in place to deal with the situations where enforcing discipline automatically is not possible.

Source code control systems are an excellent example of this: While they cannot entirely prevent programmers from overwriting the code of their team mates, they make it harder.

Even if someone deliberately messes up the work of others, the revision history still serves as a backup mechanism.

By enforcing discipline automatically, we make it easier to do things right than to do them wrong. As a result, the chances of things going wrong are greatly reduced, and work will be carried out in a more procedural manner.

Unfortunately, it is not always possible to automatically enforce a certain way of doing things, even if that way is generally accepted to be the Right Way to do them. For instance, it is understood that software systems should be documented. Yet documentation is rarely present and mostly out of date. The least we can do to ease this chore is reduce the amount of overhead to a minimum.

Depending on company policy, you may ask a developer about an undocumented system via instant messenger. Capturing these instant-messenger conversations can be a good start for documenting the system, with a minimum of added effort from either side. Although it is hardly up to professional quality standards, it is considerably better to have a captured conversation in a wiki than having no documentation at all.

12.2 Don't rely on undocumented behaviour

As we get to know the platform that we work on better and better, it gets more and more tempting to start using undocumented behaviour of that platform to get things done.

For instance, in a spreadsheet program, we may at some point 'know' that calculations are performed row by row rather than column by column, and tune our calculations accordingly. When at some point a new version of the spreadsheet is issued, or if for instance we port the spreadsheet from Excel to OpenOffice, this undocumented behaviour is subject to change.

There is nothing wrong with performing 'measurements' on a black box system to find out how it works on the inside, but if we base our code on the results, we reduce the portability of our code and increase the risk that our software system will break at the next upgrade, because we rely on undocumented behaviour.

12.3 Fix problems at the source

In medicine, treating the symptoms of a sickness may earn the pharmaceutical industry more than actually curing the disease. When given the choice, however, most people would opt for a cure, rather than a treatment. The same is true in software development. When faced with the task of fixing a bug, we have to understand the cause of the problem. Otherwise, we are merely treating symptoms, and a bug that we thought we had fixed may keep popping up.

Sometimes, the immediate cause of a bug is found (for instance a forgotten precondition check), but the actual origins are to be found in flawed design. This may for example happen when a bug has been copy/pasted to many places.

If you find such a design flaw, rather than fixing the bug in a multitude of places, in the long run it is usually better to fix the design. In the case of copy/pasted code, this can be done by defining a function, fix the bug there, and refactor the various old copies of the code to call that function instead.

If we consistently refactor flawed code to flawless code, in the long run we should end up with a flawless system. The refactoring should itself help by making that system easier to maintain, although refactoring existing systems can be a long process.

12.4 Save time by allocating enough time

Doing something wrong first and right afterwards will cost more time than doing things right the first time around.

Given this statement, we should decide how much time is enough. Depending on how experienced they are, programmers should be able to give relatively accurate estimates of how much time they will need to finish a certain task.

Nothing is more stressful to a programmer than being forced to finish a task within an unrealistic time frame. Such time frames are often the result of the marketing department making unrealistic promises to the client.

Let programmers estimate the required time themselves, and communicate this estimate with the client. Insist to the programmers that they take the responsibility to deliver as planned. Better estimates can be obtained by having multiple developers making an estimate for the same task. After a task is finished, keep a record of how long it actually took. This documentation will allow you to make more accurate estimates in the future.

When a new programmer starts on the project, a different planning is required, because different programmers solve problems in different ways. Time needed to get familiar with the used project and tools should be included in this new planning.

12.5 Plan emergencies properly

In case of a big commercial benefit or emergency, it may be interesting to go against the rules and do something the 'wrong way' before doing it right. This allows for much shorter response times, but the risk is that we will never be given the time to do things right.

To assess this risk, before implementing a quick and dirty solution, communicate with your client that although a temporary solution can be implemented very quickly, it will require a significant amount of cleaning up afterwards. During this clean-up phase, the client needs to be aware that our time is already allocated to them; it can not be allocated twice. This means that less urgent matters will have to wait.

It may be possible to implement a quick and dirty solution in a week, or a clean solution in four weeks. The full task will then take roughly five weeks. Talk to management; It may be a good idea to have the client agree that half of this amount will be charged on completion of the quick-and-dirty solution. This will help prevent the client from entering a permanent state of emergency, because quick-and-dirty work alone is most likely less cost-effective than the full solution. As the system is kept in better shape, emergencies are in turn less likely to occur.

Delivering a patch may cost more work and effort than a regular release. Make it clear to the client that patches are exclusively intended for emergencies, and thus shouldn't be used instead of the normal release cycle.

12.6 Defensive programming

Even though by convention we may have agreed that certain strings should be in lower-case, it may be that not everyone obeys by these rules.

What is called "defensive programming" by many people is actually one of the main issues that this text is about: guaranteeing preconditions. The fact that a certain string should be lower-case is a precondition, so we need to guarantee this precondition. This can be done in different ways- either by raising an error when the string is not in the correct case, or by putting the string in the correct case. Defensive programming assumes that a certain condition is wrong, and attempts to correct it before it causes trouble.

12.7 Write testable code

In a piece of code that I developed, I noticed that a certain dialog which would rarely be displayed, started popping up at the wrong moment. I noticed that the logic which decided if the dialog should pop up, was part of the code of a button which performed a file export.

Free automated testing software for C++ is hard to find, so for this hobby project, I wasn't using any. I found that the error could not be reproduced automatically, because I couldn't simulate clicking the button. I had tested the button manually, but this case had slipped through my tests.

The reason that I could not test the functionality of the button through a unit test was because the pop-up logic was an integral part of the button (known as the "*magic push button*" anti-pattern, as I found out later). Would I have written this logic as a separate function which would be called from that button, I could have written a unit test for that function[28].

I learned the hard way that the code in user interface elements should be kept as simple as possible. By keeping front end and back end separated, you will create the conditions that allow you to at least write unit tests for your code.

Some programmers go as far as writing unit tests *before* writing the code that is to be tested[29]. This will affect the way we think about writing code, because it will force us to write our code in such a manner that it can be tested automatically.

---

28 A Model-View-Controller design pattern would be worth considering, as it could allow for recording and playing back macros. This would allow for automated testing, without requiring specific software.

29 See **Write tests first**, page 275

Chapter 13

Automatic Quality Control

When code can not be made part of the system when it does not comply to certain predefined quality-standards, we will know for sure that the quality of all parts of the system will meet our standards. It is possible to meet many of these demands by means of automated checks. This has resulted in some of the highest quality software ever written.

Some thoughts on this are described next.

13.1 Catch errors in compile time

Despite all the thoroughness in the world, you may still be confronted with bugs and errors. The later you spot bugs, the more time it will take to fix them, so it is important to find errors as early as possible in the development process.

The compiler or language you use can be of tremendous assistance in finding problems in your code, provided you help your environment to help you.

Consider the following statement:

```
form.setField(
      "MyTooLongNamedAddressField",
      "North pole"
);
```

If we happen to be as unfortunate as to make a typo in the field name `MyVeryLongNamedAddressField`, sure enough the code won't work as intended. What's worse, no compiler is likely to detect this error, because it is a string between quotes. This can not be completely avoided, however there is no reason to not let the compiler help us to find typos.

What if we define the field name in a constant?

```
const ADDRESSFIELD=
            "MyTooLongNamedAddressField";
form.setField(ADDRESSFIELD,"North pole");
```

As soon as we use the field name more than once, we will start reaping the benefits:

- If we have a development environment with code completion, it will help us write the name of the constant, reducing the chance of errors in written code;

- If we compile the code, ADDRESSFIELD must exist. If we misspell it, the compiler will raise an error.

- Changing the field name later on (should this be required) will be less work.

This practice can be taken a step further. Consider the following (rather questionable[30]) code:

```
void show_dialog(string strDialogName)
{
        switch (strDialogName)
        {
                case "help":
                        show_dialog_help();
                        break;
                case "file":
                        show_dialog_file();
                        break;
                case "print":
                        show_dialog_print();
                        break;
                default:
                        throw Exception(
                        "Dialog does not exist!");
        }
}
```

---

30 The function merely seems to act as a layer of indirection. It may be possible to drop it altogether and call the individual functions directly- or to at least create an array of functions and drop the switch statement.

Usefulness of the function aside, we can define some constants that help us catch typos in the dialog names in compile time:

```
const DIALOG_HELP="help";
const DIALOG_FILE="file";
const DIALOG_PRINT="print";
```

However, this still allows us to call the function with regular strings as function parameter. As a result, we still can not guarantee the absence of typos in the parameters. In a situation like this, it is useful to use an enumerated type, for example:

```
enum DialogType
{
        DIALOGTYPE_HELP,
        DIALOGTYPE_FILE,
        DIALOGTYPE_PRINT
};


void show_dialog(DialogType diatype)
{
        switch (diatype)
        {
                case DIALOGTYPE_HELP:
                        show_help_dialog();
                        break;
                case DIALOGTYPE_FILE:
                        show_file_dialog();
                        break;
                case DIALOGTYPE_PRINT:
                        show_print_dialog();
                        break;
                default:
                        throw Exception(
                        "Dialog does not exist!");
        }
}
```

As it is now impossible to compile the code while specifying a non-existing dialog type, we've just prevented an error from ever possibly occurring in runtime.

Also, some compilers will detect when an enumerated type is used in a case statement, and will complain when not all possible values are accounted for.

Needless to say, this allows us to catch possible errors much quicker than by any means of runtime testing. Moreover, we *guarantee* that we will catch the errors, whereas in runtime we would only catch such errors by chance.

It has been common knowledge for decades that it is a best practice to not use hard coded values. Isn't it strange that after all this time, virtually every programming language still allows us to use hard coded variables without even raising compiler warnings?

In many programming languages, it is easy to accidentally substitute the comparison operator (==) for the assignment operator (=). The result is an if statement which is always evaluated as true, and which has an assignment as side effect:

```
if (b=5)
{
        /* b has just been assigned value 5
           This branch is always executed */
}
```

Some people recommend reversing the left-hand side and right-hand side of the comparison. This will force the compiler to raise an error when an assignment operator is used instead of a comparison.

The result will look as follows:

```
if (5=b)
{
    /* Assigning to left hand side
       is impossible, compile will fail */
}
```

Keep in mind that this is not a cure-all solution, as it will not catch errors where one variable is assigned the value of the other variable. The following will simply assign the value of variable b to variable a, rather than comparing the two variables:

```
if (a=b)
{
    /* switching around sides makes
       no difference to the compiler. */
}
```

Fortunately, many compilers nowadays understand that we usually do not intend to assign variables a value in the expression part of an if statement, and will raise a warning when we write something like the above.

If your compiler raises a warning in such cases, rather than switching around the arguments of an `if` expression, you may want to configure it to treat all warnings as errors. This will be a more reliable solution than depending on mere mortals to switch around the arguments of the expression.

13.2 Compile with 0 errors, 0 warnings

When our code contains syntax errors, it will not compile, and obviously we will not ship such code to our customers. Compile warnings are a different story altogether: these are non-critical errors which do not cause a compile to fail, but which are indicators that normal program operation may be disrupted.

If we are serious about the quality of our software, we want to be informed about as many potential problems as possible. Many programming environments allow you to be more picky than usual in compile time. There may be compile flags to enable all warnings, or one-liners that will tell the compiler to be more picky.

Examples that come to mind are the -Wall and -Werror options in the GNU Compiler Collection, use strict and the -w flag in Perl and Option Explicit in languages similar to Visual Basic. If you develop JavaScript and happen to use Firefox, you can set Javascript.options.strict to true on the about:config page. Find out what options your programming platform allows to make it more picky about what you write; once in place, these will help you pinpoint potential problems without any additional effort. If you develop web pages, it is highly recommended to regularly run your pages through HTML- and CSS validators to make sure they conform to existing standards.

Compile warnings mean that the code could be compiled and is syntactically correct, but that a situation has been detected that will potentially cause problems in runtime. However, warnings normally do not block compilation. As a result, warning-ridden code may end up in the production environment of the client, which of course is bad news.

Fortunately, many compilers and languages nowadays allow us to treat warnings as errors. That is, if a warning is found, the build will fail.

Enable whatever flags you can to treat warnings as errors; before long, you will be used to writing warning-free code, which is also less likely to break in runtime. This will in turn save you debugging time, causing the minimal extra effort to be earned back in a very small amount of time.

13.3 Write unit tests

A unit test is a piece of program code that checks another piece of source code for the presence of errors, by feeding it all expected sorts of input and verifying the results against a predefined answer. When the results match the expected results, the unit being tested is assumed to work as intended.

After changing a piece of code, running its unit tests will help us make sure that it keeps behaving as expected. Ideally, running the unit tests should not be a manual effort (only); it is far more useful to (also) run them during nightly build on the build server.

Other than for testing purposes, unit tests can provide us with useful examples of how to use (or not use) a piece of code.

Consider the following test code which will test one aspect of the behaviour of the `substr` function:

```
string x="abcdefghij";
dummy=substr(x,8,3); // string, start, length
if (!(dummy.equals("ij")))
{
        throw new Exception("substr(x,8,3)=='"
        +dummy+"', should be 'ij'");
}
```

This unit test shows that the programmer (who either wrote the `substr` function or simply wants to make sure that it behaves in a certain way) expects the string "ij" to be returned when the `substr` function is called with parameters "abcdefghij", 8 and 3.

This shows that the position is zero-based (the letter "i" is the ninth character in the string but has index 8), and also shows that the programmer expected this function to return the remainder of the string, should one try to read past the end of the string.

In this sense, unit tests can play a useful role in documenting code.

Unit tests may facilitate porting code from one platform to another. If another platform for instance uses a one-based starting position, the original unit test will fail. In such cases, it is possible to create a new substring function for each platform, that will work identical to the substring function on the platform for which the code was originally developed.

Unfortunately a unit test can not prove that all errors are absent; it can only prove that the tested errors are not present.

There are however certain classes of errors that are likely to occur in our code and for which we can include checks in our unit tests even before writing the actual code:

- **Undefined values:** Does the function work properly when called with undefined objects, zero values, null pointers or empty strings? If a structure or object is passed to the function, does it deal well with the absence of certain fields or properties?

- **Range boundary checks:** For numeric parameters, we deliberately call the function with values outside the normal range of operation.

What happens when we check a substring function with zero length? With negative length? With a length greater than the end of the string being processed? With a length *exactly equal* to the length of the string being processed?

- **Binary overflow and wrap-around:** For n-bit values, does the function work as expected when it is called with the values $2^{(n-1)}-1$, $2^{(n-1)}$, 2^n-1, 2^n?

- **Floating point operations:** Does the code deal well with rounding errors?

- **Object-oriented code:** Does destructing an object cause a crash? If it does, it is often due to a forgotten initialization in the object constructor.

- **Lack of Resources:** Does the code fail elegantly when it can not allocate required resources such as memory, storage space, or CPU power?

- Many other errors can be predicted. Feel free to extend this list to suit your own needs.

All these tests assume black-box testing, or testing based on the functional specification of a program. We can write tests for code without having any knowledge of the code that will be tested, or even the code itself.

If we have access to the code that is being tested, we can go a step further: We can then write a glass-box test which can go as far as testing all combinations of inputs, following all possible code paths and running all statements at least once.

If a piece of code is simple enough, we can write an exhaustive test for it. Consider the following PSD:

function hasNullObject(Object object1,Object object2, Object object3) returns bool			
object1==null?			
true	**false**		
	object2==null?		
	true	**false**	
		object3==null?	
		true	**false**
return true;			**return false;**

This piece of code has 3 input parameters, which are each of an object data type, which can in theory account for an infinite number of different states. However, the only thing that happens in the code is that the object parameters are checked for being null or not. This would indicate a total of 8 possible situations:

object1	*object2*	*object3*
null	null	null
not null	null	null
null	not null	null
not null	not null	null
null	null	not null
not null	null	not null
null	not null	not null
not null	not null	not null

Do we need al these combinations, or can we take a short cut? After all, having intimate knowledge of the code itself, we know that there are only 4 possible code paths that the computer can follow in executing the code, so why not call the function with the following parameters:

object1	object2	object3
null	(don't care)	(don't care)
not null	null	(don't care)
not null	not null	null
not null	not null	not null

This will cause every code path to be followed. As the PSD showed, in the first case, the values of both `object2` and `object3` can be disregarded. In the second case, the value of `object3` is unimportant.

The problem is in changing code. Imagine `object3` has the value `null` much more often than `object1`. To boost performance, we switch around the checks for `object3` and `object1`, and the code will run faster. However, this also changes the code paths that are followed, so the unit test will lose full code coverage and would also need to be changed along, whereas the full unit test would not have needed any alterations.

Writing a complete glass-box test may involve writing out all the possible combinations of inputs and reasoning about the desired outcome. This will give a lot of insight into the problem being solved, but may be very time consuming. As such, full glass-box tests will usually only be realistic for small modules.

When a piece of software gets sufficiently complex, it will become clear that the code can have so many different states that it becomes unrealistic to test all of them. We will then have to abandon our practice of attempting to write a piece of code that tests every possible combination of input values. Instead, whenever we encounter an error, we will try to find out which combination of conditions triggered the error, write a unit test that reproduces that scenario, and fix the code. We can then be sure that the condition won't trigger that error again.

Most of the time, unit tests will run under a unit test framework. Some well-known frameworks are *nunit* (C++), *junit* (java) and *csunit* (C#), which are all available for free. Similar modules are available for other languages.

If you wish to implement unit testing, go ahead and download one of the frameworks. Read the documentation that comes with these frameworks. The "Getting started" section (or whatever it may be called) will have you up to speed in no time.

It is important to realize that our capability to implement unit tests does not depend on these frameworks; if no unit testing framework is available for your favourite language, you can still write unit tests without one.

You should be able to make a start on unit testing in a matter of days. It is likely, however, that it will be difficult or impossible to come up with proper unit tests for existing code, especially when dealing with long functions or big modules. The reason for this is that the existing code was never written with the intention to make it testable. This is normal; you will find that your coding style will improve as you get used to writing tests along with new code.

13.4 Use automated check lists

The previous chapter gave a list of things you could check for in a unit test. By using such a list and extending it whenever we find something lacking, we can prevent a lot of problems and bugs in a very systematic manner.

Of course, merely adding items to a check-list may not be enough. For instance, a check point "Have we checked if the database design has changed?" is useless if we have no way to verify if any changes occurred, so in such a case we must first find a way to detect database design changes.

We do not want to perform all checks manually. Instead, we want to have our development environment do that for us, automatically. When it comes to quality, sometimes problems can be avoided by selecting the right programming platform before starting a project. Powerful programming languages such as C and C++ do not offer a lot of assistance in preventing problems such as memory leaks, incorrect pointer arithmetic and such, whereas other languages such as Java have no pointers and built-in garbage collection. Although this does not render the problem irrelevant, it will help reduce its impact.

Switching environments is not always an option, though. The British automobile industry was faced with the fact that they needed to program in C, but still required to produce reliable software, as safety was a priority. To address the problems associated with writing quality code in C, the MISRA (Motor Industry Software Reliability Association) set up a list of as many as 127 guidelines (which has extended since) to prevent common mistakes. These guidelines are available from the MISRA website at `http://www.misra.co.uk`, or can be found with your favourite search engine.

The interesting part is that many guidelines could be enforced automatically, and quite a few of them apply as much to C as to other languages (e.g. rule 75: "Every function shall have an explicit return type").

If checks can be performed automatically, great. This will leave less room for human error. In addition to enabling all warnings on your compiler, treating warnings as errors and using language validators, you can add your own tools to the build cycle to automatically check for certain classes of errors.

If you work in a Unix-like environment, you can call these validators to your Makefile; if you work with Visual Studio, you can set your project properties to include a post-build event which will trigger your validations. This can start with checks as simple as checking the maximum line length of your source files, up to automatically enforcing entire coding standards.

13.5 Write tests first

Once you are used to writing unit tests, start writing them *before* you write the code that has to pass those tests. This is practice is called *Test-driven development*, or more accurately *Test-first development*.

Writing your test code before the actual code being tested has a few advantages. First of all, it will force us to write code that is actually testable. The test code doubles as a formal requirement specification of the system. Being written first, it will become an integral part of the system, rather than something that is added as an afterthought, or something that will be 'forgotten' due to a tight deadline. This guarantees that we will actually *have* tests for our system.

This guaranteed presence of tests is a powerful debugging tool by itself. If new code accidentally breaks some functionality, our unit tests will give us feedback about it immediately, rather than weeks later. This will make it easier to locate and fix problems.

Finally, once we are done writing our code, it will not only be *possible* to test it, but we can confidently move on to the next piece of code, in the knowledge that the code *has been* tested and is verified to be correct (within our definition of 'correct').

Of course all this is still no guarantee that the code that we have written is bug-free. When a bug is detected, we extend our test code with code that can reproduce and detect the error condition, and then we fix the unit code so that the error condition no longer occurs. The bug in question has then been resolved and, in theory, will never come back.

13.6 Run tests as part of the compile cycle

Merely having unit tests will not guarantee that they are run. Because of this, it is a good idea to make unit tests part of the automatic nightly build of the system.

If a unit test fails on the build server during the nightly build, a lot of time is lost, because the nightly build is typically run only once every 24 hours.

Unless the time required for automatically running the tests is considerable, it is a good idea to run these tests as part of the compile cycle.

When the unit tests are made part of the compile cycle on the desktop of the programmer, the programmer will receive feedback in a much earlier stage. By running unit tests as part of the compile cycle, we no longer leave running the tests to discipline. This means that when a programmer works as before, unit tests are automatically run.

Technically, when the code compiles without errors, a post-build event can be triggered. This post-build event normally installs the compiled version for running, but it can also automatically run the unit tests. If a unit test fails, the compiled code is considered invalid. Ideally, such code is prevented from being committed to source control, turning source control into a repository of valid, tested code.

13.7 Find anti-patterns during compilation

Although we can not catch all errors, the chance that our client receives a compiled system that contains syntax errors is nearly zero; after all, if our system would contain syntax errors, it would not compile.

There are certain practices that we can follow that will further reduce the chance of errors. Let us take another look at the piece of code from the paragraph **Verify Preconditions** (page 77):

```
int a(object object1)
{
    int x=object1.getobject2().getvalue();
    return x;
}
```

The expression `object1.getobject2().getvalue()` contains more than one dot, which implies that the value of a method or property (in this case the result of `getobject2()`) is not checked.

It is certainly possible to write a validator that detects such expressions. Likewise, it is possible to write a validator that will detect that variable `object1` is used without having been checked for having a `null` value.

Effectively, when we add such validations to our compile cycle, what we are doing is limiting what we consider valid syntax.

We can write code that detects a wide variety of problems, and add these checks to our compile cycle. If our code does not adhere to the coding standards that we set, it will fail to compile, indicating that our code contains problems.

All of these problems are detected at compile time, before we even have started testing. All these little extensions add up, resulting in a 'safer' programming environment which will force us into a more disciplined style of programming. In turn, this leads to code which contains fewer bugs.

We can go pretty far in this, as is demonstrated by the SPARK ADA programming language. Spark ADA is a safe subset of ADA intended to write high integrity software (for use in airliners, medical equipment, etc.) where the highest possible quality standards are needed (CMM level 5 or better[31]).

SPARK Ada is limited in such a way that common errors are impossible to code. For instance, SPARK ADA does not allow heap allocation, pointers nor recursion.

As a result, memory requirements can be predicted and stack overflows can not occur. In addition, SPARK ADA is an annotated subset of regular ADA. It allows the programmer to add design-by-contract information inside comments. These allow an additional toolset to analyze if the code written matches the specification in the comments.

Our set of syntax validating extensions ultimately perform the same function as this toolset.

31The Capability Maturity Model only has 5 levels. Sometimes a defect rate better than typically achieved with CMM level 5 is required.

13.8 Equip your system with a self-test

It is a good idea for a program to execute some type of diagnostics to test its own consistency when it is started. This will help detect problems and solve them before they happen. Detecting errors during such a self test also speeds up manual testing, because if a mistake is caught during program start-up, this saves us the work of transcending half the program. It is all right for such a self test to take a few seconds, as it is executed only once during program start-up[32]. If it would be performed during operation of the program, the same test might get in the way.

Possible targets for such a self-test are for instance issues that have to do with configuration:

- Do all specified directories exist?

- Is the database server up and running?

- If the program plays audio, is a sound card detected?

- Are the amount of available disk space or memory likely to become a problem?

These are often issues that do not need verifying over and over again. If a directory doesn't exist, we can create it and lock it so that no other process can remove it anymore. If no sound card is detected, it is not usually very likely that one will suddenly be present from one moment to another, so we can default to a dummy audio driver that does not require a sound card.

---

32 This may be an appropriate time to think of adding a splash screen.

When a system depends on manually edited text files that are parsed during execution, a typo can cause the program to fail. Is it possible to check for typos by comparing one file to another? If we can automatically detect such problems during program start-up, this will save us quite a bit of time spent on bug-hunting.

Whenever the system fails, we should ask ourselves if this problem could have been resolved or detected during a self-test. If so, we add it to the self test module of the system. Obviously, which self tests can be performed on a system varies from one system to another.

13.9 Let the system keep a log

At times we may be confronted with bug reports from users that have no idea that they were doing something wrong, or that are ashamed of an action that they performed which may have resulted in data loss. At times like these, if there are problems with the system, we will not be able to count on our users for troubleshooting, as they may be unable or unwilling to tell us what the cause of the problem is.

In turn, we are unable to reproduce the problematic behaviour of the system, and a status quo is born.

Having a system log can then be a great help in troubleshooting problems. When the system log is sufficiently detailed, we can exactly follow the flow of actions that a user performed that led to an error condition. If the user says that "suddenly the data was gone" and the system log clearly shows that the user selected 10 records, pressed 'delete' and confirmed the removal of said records, we will know that the problem existed between chair and computer, rather than in our software system.

This page intentionally left blank

Chapter 14

Working with databases

There are various ways to store data: ISAM, CSV files, XML or binary files. But when it comes to ease of querying, maintainability and extendibility, SQL-based databases are still by far the most popular choice, despite their relatively poor handing of relationships and sub-typing[33].

This chapter will not deal with database design, which was already covered in chapter 4, but it will go a bit more in depth about some practical aspects of working with SQL databases.

---

33 See chapter **Software Architecture**, page 43 and further

14.1 Choose (non-)standard SQL

I was introduced to MySQL when I started programming for the web. I had been working with Oracle for some time, and I found that table joins such as the following no longer worked:

```
SELECT person.name, dept.name
FROM person,dept
WHERE (p.dept_id=d.dept_id);
```

Initially I blamed MySQL for not being powerful enough to support table joins. As it turned out, I was wrong. The reason that table joins did not work wasn't because they were not supported, but because the above query was was written in an Oracle-centric dialect of SQL. The query worked fine after rewriting it to standard SQL:

```
SELECT person.name, dept.name
FROM person
LEFT JOIN dept
     ON (p.dept_id=d.dept_id)
WHERE (p.dept_id=d.dept_id);
```

Over time, I found myself building database-driven websites that worked with various different databases, depending on what the customer happened to have available. Instead of managing several code bases for the various database management systems used by my web development framework, it seemed to make more sense to make my SQL work equally well on MySQL, PostgreSQL, SQLServer, and Oracle. The only way that this could reasonably be accomplished was by following the SQL-92 dialect of SQL (an official standard). In my case, as the database logic for most websites is relatively straightforward, it paid off to write standard SQL only.

As it turns out, there are some relatively dramatic differences between the various database management systems. What is called `int` on one DBMS is called `integer` on another, what is called `number` on one DBMS is called `float` or `real` on another, each system has their own way of handling date and time, and so on. The `varchar` data type seems to be the only one supported natively by most any dialect of DDL[34].

If you happen to run into a database where almost any field, be it number, date or keys, are defined as `varchar` (such as on the product that was formerly called RedHat Interchange), do not immediately consider it bad design; most likely it was designed to be defined by DBMS independent DDL.

Because it is a hairy business to design for full DBMS independence, I cannot recommend anyone to write only SQL-92 for anything moderately complex.

This doesn't mean, however, that getting familiar with SQL-92 is a futile effort. It will make *you* more flexible in moving between different databases. Also, if you adhere to SQL-92 whenever you can, your application will be easier to port to other DBMS platforms than applications built for a single DBMS-specific dialect.

Likewise, it pays off to be conservative with special characters, mixed case, reserved words and spaces in tables and column names, as not every DBMS will handle them gracefully.

---

34 DDL is the SQL Data Definition Language by which the structure of databases is defined.

14.2 Keep database tables narrow

Tables that span dozens of columns are often an indication of a poorly normalized database[35]. As a rule of the thumb, try to keep the size of all database tables at 7 columns or less, if possible.

Usually, when a table has many columns, it can be replaced with a table that has few columns and more rows. There are generally two situations that cause many columns in a table:

- Attempting to store several child-items in a table; for instance, in a table person, the table would contain columns for `child1name`, `child2name`, `child3name`, `child1birthdate`, `child2birthdate` and so on; this should be avoided, because it implies logical limitations and will make it more cumbersome to query the database. Instead, a table for the children could be created - or, in this case, the children could be stored as entries in the table `person` with a reference to the key of the records of their parents.

- Attempting to store an ever-expanding list of properties in a table; for instance, for a table `contactinfo`, the table would contain columns for phone number, cell phone, fax number, email address, secondary email address, MSN address, and so on. This list can keep growing infinitely and requires a developer to make each change.

---

35 See chapter **Software Architecture**, page 43 and further

From a maintainability perspective, it makes more sense to create table that contains one record for each type of contact information, and another table that contains the actual contact information, with a foreign key pointing to the person record that the contact information belongs to, or link the two tables together with a third one[36].

This allows the system to be maintained by an application administrator, rather than by you as a developer. As a result, you will save precious time, and your customer will save money.

---

36 See "**Keep data structures normalized**", page 68

14.3 Use parameterized queries

Whenever we run SQL queries from our program code, there is a good chance that our code sends multiple similar queries to the DBMS. In other situations, the WHERE clause of our query will contain some data that is entered by our users.

The naïve approach in both situations is to construct a string containing the query to be sent to the database server. But this is not the best way to deal with programmatically constructed queries.

Whenever we send multiple similar queries, this requires the database client to construct the query string over and over again, after which it is sent to the database server which then has to parse and execute (almost) the same query over and over again as well. But if we can construct a single query and reuse it without change, the database client can save itself some work constructing query strings. The following code is a PHP example of this:

```
$db=pg_connect("dbname=mydatabase");
$myprep=pg_prepare($db,"prep",
     "DELETE FROM employees WHERE dept=$1");
$depts=array("development","sales",
          "Jim's department");
foreach ($depts as $currdep) {
     $result=pg_execute($db,"prep",$currdep);
}
```

There is a vast number of different implementations of parameterized queries, and implementation details will vary depending on programming language and DBMS used, but the general concept is identical.

Depending on implementation, using parameterized queries will help the database server to easily detect that the query being sent has been issued recently.

As a result of this, the database server may decide that the query string does not need to be re-parsed, improving performance on the server side as well. Some network bandwidth may be saved, if the design of client and server is clever enough: the client can then simply tell the server to reuse the previously prepared parameterized query with new parameter values, instead of re-sending the entire query.

In the code above, note that the parameter `$1` in the parameterized query is not surrounded by quotes. The `prepare` statement takes care of this, and will also make sure that any special characters (such as the apostrophe in the last array element) are automatically escaped as needed, making our system less sensitive to SQL injection attacks.

14.4 Keep the Cartesian Product small

When your need to join several tables to collect a certain data set, it is very likely that the DBMS engine will generate all possible combinations of records from one table with another. Thus, if you join 3 tables of 10 records, the Cartesian product of the tables already contains 10 x 10 x 10 = 1000 combinations of records. Because of this, a query such as the following will most likely not run very fast:

```
SELECT person.name,
       department.dept_name,
       salary.amount
FROM person
LEFT JOIN department
     ON (person.dept=department.id)
LEFT JOIN salary
     ON (person.id=salary.pers_id)
WHERE (person.name='Dilbert')
AND (department.dept_name='Engineering');
```

By reducing the amount of records per subset, the size of the Cartesian product will dramatically be reduced, and as a result, the query will potentially run much faster. We can accomplish this by adding the parts that are in the WHERE clause to the relevant ON clauses, as demonstrated in the following query. As you will see, writing such a query is hardly any more difficult than the poorly performing one above.

```
SELECT person.name,
       department.dept_name,
       salary.amount
FROM person
LEFT JOIN department
     ON (person.dept=department.id
         AND person.name='Dilbert'
         AND department.dept_name
             = 'Engineering'
     )
LEFT JOIN salary
     ON (person.id=salary.pers_id
         AND person.name='Dilbert'
     )
WHERE (person.name='Dilbert')
AND (department.dept_name='Engineering');
```

Depending on the DBMS used, this may significantly boost the performance of your queries. On others, the effect will be less dramatic.

The Cartesian product is now much reduced, but it may still take quite a bit of time to construct the subsets themselves. By making sure that an index is kept for the columns being queried, constructing the subsets will be substantially more efficient.

This is of course just the tip of the iceberg when it comes to SQL performance optimization. Entire volumes have been written on the subject, and this text won't be able to replace those volumes.

For more tips and tricks about SQL performance tuning, consult the appropriate books.

14.5 Keep data values out of program code

When working with legacy systems, I have regularly encountered the programming practice of using database values (often key values) in program conditions, such as

```
if (company_key=='1352')
{
    // do something specific to this company
    // (often values such as 9999 appear;
    // this is just as random as 1352)
}
```

In other words, the program code attaches a special meaning to certain keys. There are multiple problems associated with storing information in program code:

- It may introduce a 'time bomb' in the system: in the above example, a problem may arise when a table hits 1352 (or 9999) records.

- Reduced separation of business logic and database. Extra code may be needed to filter 'special' keys when querying the table, all of which needs to contain each 'special' key.

- Makes it substantially harder to re-populate the database from scratch, should the need ever arise. When the database is being repopulated, new keys may need to be assigned; This means all code needs to be checked as well.

We can overcome these problems by defining an additional field in the table which indicates that the record has the given special meaning. The name of the column can then be used to give a clue about what that special meaning is. Alternatively, an entire table can be devoted to the purpose, containing references to all records with the given special meaning.

We can then write reusable, low-maintenance program code that performs certain actions if any of these 'special records' is encountered; but it is the database, rather than the program code, that holds the information about which records are the special ones.

A configuration tool can be created to allow the customer to maintain which records are supposed to have the desired 'special' meaning.

14.6 Explicitly name your columns

When writing SQL queries for programmatic use, you should explicitly list the names of the columns that you intend to receive, rather than performing a SELECT * query. There are several reasons for this:

- SELECT * will address all columns in all tables that you are trying to access. Unless you actually need all of them, this will result in unnecessary performance loss and increased memory usage.

- By explicitly naming which columns you want to retrieve, you will have control over the order in which the query returns the columns to you- even if the database design changes.

- When the order of the columns in the result is known, you can access them by a numeric index. This is likely to perform better than having to look up the columns by their name.

Of course, when accessing a database manually, rather than programmatically, these reasons may not be as important.

14.7 Access data via an interface

When designing a database, we will be faced with a data structure and operations that can be performed on that data structure. As this is consistent with object-oriented programming, it makes sense to treat the database as such.

Rather than having all your code directly perform queries on the database, consider writing an interface layer that always handles all data access.

There are several benefits to writing such interface code:

- In the case of complex transactions across various tables, interface code will be simpler to understand because your fellow programmers will not need to know the implementation details of your code to work with it.

- It helps you centralize code. Therefore, if the database structure changes, most likely you will only need to change the appropriate functions in the interface code; but most likely not the code that uses it.

There are basically two possibilities for implementing such interface functions:

- As stored procedure in the DBMS

- As wrapper class used by the Business Logic Layer of your system

An example will help clarify things. For instance, to add a user, we can create a function `add_user(username,password)`. This function may perform a complex transaction which consists of the following:

- create an entry in the user table;

- encrypt the password using the default encryption scheme (possibly based on a setting in the configuration table);

- add the user to the default user groups, and

- assign the default set of roles to the user.

Perhaps in our system, all of these operations must be carried out to create a valid user entry. By providing an interface function to create the user, our fellow programmers are no longer bothered by implementation details for creating a user.

Providing interface functions to read data from and write data to a database will help us see a database in a more object-oriented manner.

Should the password table be separated from the main user table for whatever reason (a fundamental change in the database structure), we can simply modify the existing function to work with multiple tables, whereas any code using the original `add_user` function can stay the way it was before.

14.8 Use informationless keys

For maintaining referential integrity within your database, use informationless, structure free keys as primary key for your tables.

A good example of an informationless key is a UUID (essentially a random 128 bit value, guaranteed to be unique) which is typically displayed as hex string. Such a key may not look very friendly to the user. That is because it is not intended to be displayed to the user[37]- it is intended for the computer.

We distinguish between keys that are used for maintaining referential integrity and keys that have some meaning to the user, or contain some information.

A user may use his or her email address as username; when this username or email address is used to maintain referential integrity between the various tables, many tables need to be updated when the user wants a different username. Most likely, the user will need to logout or access needs to be temporarily blocked in the process of changing username, as the database transaction implied by a username change is considerable.

In contrast, when referential integrity between tables is maintained by an informationless key rather than by the username, the user can readily change email address as it only implies changing a single field in one record in the database. As a result, changing the username is a minimal change.

---

37 See chapters **Preventing chaos** and **Use UUIDs where appropriate** (pages 59, 62) for a deeper explanation about informationless keys.

If you relate records from two or more tables into another table, rather than using a combination of multiple keys to identify the record, it is a good idea to create a new, informationless, one-column key to identify this relation. This ensures that one field is always enough to identify your records.

In turn, this will prevent a lot of the maintenance that you would otherwise spend re-keying tables (and perhaps rewrite associated code) to restore referential integrity when an additional key column is added to the table (usually when an additional table is joined into the relation).

Another benefit of giving each record a database-wide unique, one-field key, is that all keys in the database share the same structure- they are compatible with each other.

This high degree of compatibility will prove useful if you want to record information that needs to transcends the structure of the records being referenced. This occurs, for instance, when you want to keep a change history of records (of any type), or if you want to store access control information for records (of any type).

If all keys of all records consist of a one-column key, you can create a table containing information about any record type by using a single key column to reference all those different record types, and perhaps a second column to indicate in which table each record is stored. This is relatively simple to implement- but imagine what a mess it would be to build such functionality if each table in your database would has a different key structure!

Chapter 15

Security considerations

Imagine that the software that you write is like the house that you live in. If you own a lot of expensive goods, but leave the doors and windows of your house wide open, burglars will find their efforts to be paid back generously. If your house is empty, but equipped with a full-blown burglar detection and capturing system, this will likely solve most of your burglary problems[38].

In computer systems, the same applies, but instead of goods we protect information. The value of the information being protected increases as more money, more sensitive information and more users are involved.

---

38 Unless, of course, you run into the type of burglar that is interested in stealing your burglar detection and capturing system, for the sake of showing that it can be done.

The reason that we should worry about security is that security breaches can cause substantial damage to the victim. This damage manifests itself as lost time, lost money and tainted reputation. Who would trust a bank with their money, if the computer systems of that bank were known to be insecure?

This chapter is not a full blown course in computer security, but it does address some common pitfalls that I have ran into over the years. Although applying the tips and tricks in this chapter should give your systems a minimum level of security, this may not be enough for your purposes. If you are serious about security, you should consult several dedicated books on the subject, not just this chapter.

15.1 Avoid security through obscurity

When you leave your house and lock the door, do you leave the key in the flower pot or under the doormat? If you do, you are practising security through obscurity. If you always leave the key under the doormat, someone is bound to find out. You may need to tell it to your babysitter, who in turn might tell her boyfriend. Or maybe a clumsy mail man stumbling over the doormat reveals the key. But it may well be that your house is visited by a burglar who has found keys under doormats before.

In computer software, the same is true. A system that depends on people keeping their mouth shut about how security is enforced, depends on security through obscurity. Applications designed in such a way have a fundamental design flaw: They provide everything that is needed to break into them. This means that anyone with access to the application and enough determination might be able to gain unauthorized access.

An employee that leaves the company might leak information. Perhaps he or she will tell around that to get into superuser mode, you need to use a special key combination. If that key combination is hard-coded into the application itself, that version of the application is permanently compromised. As such, if you require to change the code of your application to secure it, this should raise a few eyebrows.

Instead, we should design our system security in such a way, that even having all design information of the security system will not gain us instant[39] access to the system that is being protected.

---

39 Time is an important factor in computer security. Most security systems are easily broken if we are willing to spend the billions of years needed to try all possible keys.

15.2 Be aware of ways to bypass security

Imagine you have a bullet proof, stainless steel safe door as the front door to your house, and you always take the only key with you. You may think that burglars will have a hard time forcing the door open, but it is more likely that they will simply break a window.

When a security mechanism is properly designed, efforts to break it will fail. Therefore, it makes more sense for malicious hackers[40] to work around it. To avoid getting caught, they will prefer non-intrusive ways to get what they want.

Your software possibly has a login dialog; will it secure your system if a malicious hacker installs a key-logger? Your software possibly sends data across a network; is it encrypted, or will a malicious hacker be able to analyze the data stream?

Does a potential cracker even need to run your application at all to get what (s)he wants? Your application may reside on another server than the one that contains the data. Can a malicious hacker gain access to the database server and simply look at the data? What if the server is stolen?

What if someone simply buys the drives of the server second-hand off of his preferred auction website in a few years? Will it still be possible to extract valid credit card numbers from those drives then?

---

40 'Hackers' are individuals that like to stretch the possibilities of software systems by studying them. A minority of hackers breaks into systems; they are called 'crackers', but this term never caught on. To show the bad intentions of crackers, I will refer to them as 'malicious hackers'.

15.3 Never trust user input

Most users that will ever use your software are just interested in using your software as it was intended. Some people out there, however, like to deliberately mess up things. If you're lucky, they do this just for the kick of it; if you're not, they are trying to break your software to get access to information or functionality that they should not be able to have.

The following example shows one way they might accomplish this. Let's say that we have written a web application, in which we use the following input field:

```
<input type="text" name="firstname" maxlength=10>
```

A malicious but clever user opens this page and decides to save it with menu option `file->save` in his browser. This user then opens the saved file in a text editor, alters the `maxlength` value in the saved file to `15`, and re-opens the modified file in his browser. It is now possible for the user to enter a `firstname` which is 15 characters long and submit it to the server. If there was any Javascript on the page to validate the length of the field, it can be disabled just as easily.

Although this example deals with a web page, the same lesson applies to client/server programming in general: We have no control over our users, but we do have control over our servers.

Therefore, in any client/server environment, user input should be validated *at least* on the server. If the user input is validated on the client side at all, is should be to help the responsiveness of the application, rather than for security reasons.

Some programmers try to protect themselves from unwanted user actions by using some client-side Javascript to disable access to those actions. In this case, for instance, they might disable the Save menu used by our malicious user, or disable browser menus that would pop up when right-clicking the mouse. This may seem like a good idea, but is ultimately fruitless. Not only are there many ways to get to the source code of a page, but ultimately all Javascript can be bypassed. Rather than wasting our time trying to establish security on the client side (which is ultimately beyond our control), we should get it right on the server side.

Back to our input field. Assuming we truncate the field to the desired length on the server, we still have to deal with the actual content of the field. Some characters may not be desirable as field input.

It is thinkable that the data submitted by the user is used in an SQL query that is generated by a script, for example:

```
$query="select password "
."from users "
."where firstname='".$firstname."'";
```

If the user has a normal name, all is fine. But if the user is called O'Brian, the query will result in the following, invalid SQL statement:

```
select password
from users
where firstname='O'Brian';
```

A user could enter this name and would run into an error. To malicious users, this error would be enough information to know that this system is vulnerable to SQL injection attacks.

What happens during an SQL injection attack is that a malicious user enters information in such a way, that it alters the behaviour of the system beyond its original design. For example, if the user enters this as first name:

```
' or firstname like '%
```

the resulting query would become:

```
select password
from users
where firstname='' or firstname like '%';
```

which obviously returns passwords for all users, rather than password for a single user. Depending on how the system evaluates success or failure, this might allow a malicious user to gain access to the system.

One way to prevent these problems is by filtering out or escaping all unwanted characters. But in any case, we shouldn't use user input without verifying its contents.

It is notable that this type of attack is not just limited to SQL; in any UNIX-like environment, the back-tick operator (the ` character, ASCII code 96) may give the user access to command line operations. Likewise, input redirection characters < and > are suspect.

Although code injection attacks can be quite serious, they would seem to be easy to counter by letting the server filter all user input to only allow the characters that we want to permit in it.

But filtering alone might not do: Sometimes, we *want* the user to be able to enter names such as O'Hara. Of course, we *could* escape the unwanted characters, but sometimes this is not worth the effort.

As it turns out, most of the time we want to filter the user input because it is going to be used in SQL statements. In that case, simply using parameterized queries is best, as it takes care of filtering and escaping any user input as needed.

It is important to realize that SQL injection is not the only risk of using unfiltered input; whenever user input is displayed on a web page, we must make sure to escape special characters.

Failing to do so may allow a malicious hacker to inject JavaScript in our HTML output (using the HTML `<script>` tag) in a similar way as SQL injection. These scripts may collect information about the user in several ways and send that information to the website of the malicious hacker. Due to the way they work, these Cross-site scripting (XSS) attacks also effectively bypass any firewalls. Needless to say, this technique is most effective if malicious hackers manage to save their script in the database of a frequently visited site, and having it displayed to a lot of users. It won't work, however, if we make sure to properly sanitize our user input.

15.4 Avoid clear-text passwords

Using clear-text (unencrypted) passwords is like leaving the keys to your house in plain sight- it is worse than leaving your keys under the doormat. If clear-text passwords are stored in a database, anyone with access to that database has access to all passwords. If the database password itself is stored as clear text in source code or configuration file, a glance at that source or configuration will reveal that password and permit the user to corrupt the database at will.

Using an unencrypted password in a configuration file is especially serious when this configuration file can be accessed by several people. Does your web application share a web server with other people? Surely the permissions of the configuration file are set to allow it to be read by the web server. Another user may be able to write a script that displays the configuration file of your site. You didn't hard-code the database username and password into your web application, did you?

If you did, you are not alone. It is actually a bit tricky to keep the database password out of your application, because the application needs it to work. Encoding the password is not much use, because the application also needs to be able to decode it; and the decoding algorithm needs to be present in the code.

Instead, in this case the security should be implemented on the database level. The database should only grant read access to the account represented by the username and password contained by the application. Moreover, this read access should be restricted to public information and the user base. This allows the web browsing public access to any and all information that they need to access while allowing us to restrict access to sensitive information.

What if we want to give users more elevated privileges? One way is to use the login data of the user as a decryption key.

Whenever a user tries to log in, we can use the password that they entered as a key to decrypt their personal encrypted copy of the account information required for elevated access. Whenever users change their password, this account information is re-encrypted so that only the new password can decrypt it.

I'll leave it up to you whether this account information unlocks the entire database to the web application, or if it uses the access control mechanism of the DBMS itself to restrict access.

We should be aware that users may forget their password, rendering their account information impossible to decrypt. This is no problem when a copy of the account information exists, only available to users with elevated access rights, such as database administrators. This allows the database administrators to reset the password, without ever needing to know what the password is.

Although this technique does not entirely prevent storing passwords in code, the damage that can be done with them is greatly reduced; after all, any passwords in code will only grant access to a very limited area of the database.

15.5 Use one-way password encryption

It is obvious that storing passwords as readable text is a bad idea. We can not always escape the need of storing passwords or their representations; as such, we need to encode the password in some way before storing it.

By all means, we should avoid trivial encodings such as storing the password backwards, storing it as a hex string, storing it as base64 encoded string, using a XOR mask or performing ROT13 translation. Even without source code of the password encoder, such encoding methods are easily recognized and inverted.

Instead, they should be encoded in such a way that they cannot be decoded anymore. Such one-way encryption is no problem during a login procedure; When the user enters a password, this password is encoded according to the same encoding scheme as the stored password, compared to the stored password. If they match, the user has access to the system.

An easy way to perform one-way password encoding is to generate an MD5 hash of a password[41]. Many languages already contain an MD5 library; creating an MD5 hash of a password is often something along the lines of

```
encodedpassword=MD5(password);
```

As using a hash implies that some of the input data is lost, it cannot be reversed.

---

41 Should MD5 be cracked by the time you read this, feel free to substitute your favourite secure hash algorithm.

Although theoretically several combinations of characters can result in the same hash, the chance of accidentally running into one that works is minimal; a brute force attack to crack a 128-bit hash requires on average 2^{127} attempts. If we would be able to calculate one million of such hashes per second, it would still take us, on average, 50000000000000000000000 years to crack one password. By the time we manage, said password probably won't be of much value to us anymore.

In practice, cracking such hashes can be done in considerably less time. If the 128-bit MD5 hash of a password is the string `827ccb0eea8a706c4c34a16891f84e7b`, how do you find the password if you're in a hurry? You simply look it up with your favourite search engine, and you're in.

Likewise, if we have a list of encoded passwords and we find two equal encodings, we will know that both people have the same password. This is a potential security hole: if we know the janitor has the same password as the CEO, we might be able to offer the janitor a candy bar in exchange for CEO privileges[42].

In the UNIX world, this problem was solved long ago by adding a 'salt' to the password. A 'salt' is a number or short string of characters, which are randomly chosen. The salt is added to the password before encoding it. As a result, the chance that equal passwords result in the same encoding is extremely small. As the encoded password cannot be decoded, there is no way to find people sharing the same password.

---

42 According to a survey of the the BBC in April 2004, more than 70% of people would reveal their password in exchange for a bar of chocolate.

In code, one way of adding a salt might look as follows:

```
randomize(timer);
salt=(1000000*random()).toString();
encodedpassword=salt+","+MD5(salt+password);
```

This allows us to figure out the salt by looking at the encoded password, which permits us to encode a password in the same manner as the original. In the above case, there is a one in a million chance that two people that share the same password also share the same hash. If this is not acceptable, we can verify for this possibility before our salted password is stored- and simply try again.

Of course it is still possible to perform a dictionary attack on the password list, but every attempt will need to be encoded against all salts in use by the system. Common measures such as requiring a minimal password length and mixed alphabetic/numeric characters help protect against this.

15.6 Be aware of sniffing

In designing secure software, you should assume that data that is sent through a computer network can be intercepted by the routers that route your network traffic, and by any computer on any LAN that your data passes through. Passively looking at network data without changing anything is called *sniffing*. As the data on the network itself is unaffected, sniffing is undetectable.

On Unix-like systems, a network analysis program called `tcpdump` allows people to look at incoming network data; On Windows, the functional equivalent is called `windump`.

As you run `tcpdump` on a LAN, you may find out that a lot more data is received by your computer than just the data intended for you. But you will also find out that a lot of the data that your computer sends, is not encrypted. Surprisingly, as this text is being written, encrypted network data is not the norm.

Some popular sites even have an encrypted login procedure, but then proceed the session without encryption. This is rather silly if you ask me- the point of passwords is to gain access to the data behind them. Why bother cracking a password if the data protected by it can simply be sniffed? By the way- when you receive emails with your password in plain text, you may want to reset that password to something else.

For software developers, the lesson to learn is that we should be aware that people may be listening in to the data traffic. When your application needs to send or receive sensitive data such as passwords or credit card information, it is a good idea to make sure that the data in question is sent in encrypted form. Any password-protected data should also be considered sensitive- otherwise, why bother about a password?

15.7 Avoid buffer overflows

A buffer overflow occurs when write operations to memory exceed the size allocated for a buffer.

Overwriting memory beyond the end of the buffer will leave the memory in a corrupt state, normally leading to unpredictable system behaviour.

With a considerable amount of knowledge about the defective program and the operating system, a program may be fed with input that causes a buffer overflow. When the input is well thought out, it even allows a malicious hacker to crash the program in a predictable manner. This allows malicious hackers to use buffer overflows to their advantage. By carefully crafting the input, malicious hackers manage to crash the program in such a way that it performs a task that is useful to them.

Although buffer overflow attacks require a cracker to invest some time in research, the payback may be worth the effort: When successful, it may allow full control over the machine that is being attacked.

Buffer overflow attacks are mostly a problem to low-level languages that do not perform automated bounds checking, such as assembly, C and C++.

Programs written in virtual-machine based languages (C#, Java, etc.) and most interpreted languages will generally be safer from buffer overflow attacks, although a buffer overflow may still raise exceptions or run-time errors that could terminate such programs.

How to prevent buffer overflows in low-level languages?

- Whenever we write to the buffer, we perform checks to make sure that the boundaries are not exceeded;

- We check all user input. In this case, the input can be any incoming data; it may well be a packet of network data received by the program.

- When programming in C or C++, whenever possible, use size-controlled equivalents of functions that deal with buffers, such as `strncpy` instead of `strcpy`. Also, it is best to refrain from using functions that allow user input of unlimited length such as `scanf` in the C programming language.

As operating system manufacturers are starting to take security more seriously, they have added some randomness to the memory manager, causing modules to be loaded at less predictable places in memory. This makes it harder for attackers to use the operating system itself to their advantage.

15.8 Add a bit of chaos

A lot of successful security breaches are the result of crackers being able to make correct predictions or assumptions about the system being compromised.

In the previous chapter, we learned how moving around modules randomly in memory could make it more difficult to exploit buffer overflows, because modules would no longer be at predictable locations in memory.

When money is involved, it pays to up our level of paranoia a notch. Although total security is an illusion, we can make it considerably more difficult to break security by introducing some chaos in our system.

Consider a malicious hacker that records all our keystrokes: our username, password, everything. When we visit our online banking website, it becomes clear how randomness serves us.

My bank requires me to enter a different transaction code for each online transfer that I make. With this added randomness, key logging is effectively useless, because all codes being logged are invalidated the minute that they have been used.

Something similar is being done for credit cards: For online use, credit card issuers now issue credit card numbers which are valid for one transaction only. This alone would not help much if the numbers would be issued in a predictable order. Obviously, some randomness helps security here too, because it makes it impossible (or at least very hard) to guess what the next credit card number will be, based on the last one that was used.

15.9 Treat sensitive information carefully

Every now and then, the news reports how thousands of credit card numbers were stolen by malicious hackers.

This is surprising, considering the fact that to run a web shop that accepts credit card payments, that web shop never needs to receive credit card information to validate the payment- much less to store that information.

Instead, the payment should be handled directly by a credit card payment gateway such as provided internationally by companies such as ProtX, Ogone and RedUnicre. All your website sends to your customer is a transaction number. After using this transaction number to handle the payment with the payment gateway, the customer (or the browser of the customer) will indicate to your web shop that the transaction is complete. After your web shop verifies the transaction with the payment gateway, we know that the payment was successful. As we never even received a credit card number, we can't accidentally expose this information to malicious hackers.

Whenever possible, prevent the need to transfer or store sensitive information. If you send out emails containing passwords or credit card numbers, a sniffer may be able to intercept that information. In contrast, such an email might only contain a URL. If that URL is fitted with a login screen that requires the user give a username *and* a code previously received via SMS and/or postal services, it is far less likely that a malicious hacker has been able to collect all the information required to access the actual data.

15.10 Don't rely on software alone

You may have spent considerable time on securing your software, but this is worthless without physical security.

Without physical security, it becomes nearly impossible to secure your software- because somehow your software will have to know how to get to all the data that it manages.

Someone might 'borrow' a backup tape or simply steal a server that contains sensitive information. Someone that simply sits down at the keyboard of a server will likely be able to access data that is available locally on the server but not accessible via the network.

The human factor should also not be underestimated: people often use the same passwords on multiple websites, rarely change their passwords, use passwords that are too easy to guess. Some people are simply a bit naïve and will easily be conned into giving away sensitive information.

Being aware of these issues does not make your software any better. But if you are not aware of them, the security of your software will be at stake, regardless of how well-written your code is.

This page intentionally left blank

Chapter 16

Programming for the web

This text would not be complete without some tips specifically aimed at web programming. Web programming may seem simple, but is not to be taken lightly: it is the current state of the art. Most people can learn how to build static web pages for their friends and family in a relatively short amount of time, but this is a far cry from mission-critical, multi-user, database-driven, multi-server, load-balanced, cross-browser, secure, interactive websites- looking as unimpressive as your favourite search engine.

Numerous books have been written on web development, so this chapter will only provide a few key points that have proven themselves over and over again. I hope they will be useful in your next browser-based project.

16.1 First of all, get the basics right

When programming for the web, we should consider how the web turned into existence. At the basis of the World Wide Web lay two important building blocks: HTTP (the HyperText Transfer Protocol) and HTML (the HyperText Markup Language). The combination of these two gives you the power to functionally do almost anything that the web has to offer, and even the simplest of browsers will support both of them.

A key concept in web design is *graceful degradation.* HTML was designed in such a way that a fall-back mechanism can be provided in case a browser does not support a given feature. For instance, if a browser does not support images, an alternative text can be displayed instead, such as the company name instead of the company logo:

```
<img src="http://myserver/images/companylogo.png"
     alt="ACME enterprises, Ltd.">
```

This will provide a text alternative in case loading the image should fail; it will also help to make your site more accessible to the visually impaired who may access the site through the use of text-to-speech technology.

To build dynamic web applications, the content of pages can be generated on-the-fly on the server side; this does not require additional features on the client side.

The benefit of limiting ourselves to the basics first, is that we will force ourselves to pick up proper design habits, such as performing form input validation on the server-side. This gives us a solid foundation that will make our application work on any browser.

Browsers are generally fairly forgiving in parsing human-made HTML. As different browsers forgive different mistakes, our HTML may render differently on different browsers. Our best bet for seeing our HTML rendered properly on as many browsers as possible, is to make sure that it conforms to official standards.

To validate our HTML against existing standards, we can use the tools that are available online. My personal favourite is the validator on `http://www.htmlhelp.com`. Apart from providing an excellent validation service for HTML, it also provides descriptions of the different versions of the HTML standard, style sheet validation and more.

After having validated a few files, you will find yourself writing better HTML already.

16.2 Keep core dependencies to a minimum

Once we've got the basics right, we can make our websites fancier and more responsive by using additional technologies such as Javascript, CSS style sheets, Flash, Java and browser-specific features. As we extend our site, we should be aware of the concept of graceful degradation, so that all functionality that the site has to offer is available to all browsers.

But why would we want to spend the extra time on a clunky, old-fashioned HTML-based site, if we can go fancy with Javascript straight away? Here's why. All too often, when we view the source of websites, we see code such as the following[43]:

```
<a onclick="javascript:document.location='x.htm'">
    Click here to go to document x
</a>
```

Why on earth would someone in his right state of mind want to create a link like that? There are plenty of things wrong with this approach:

- First of all, Javascript is much less forgiving to bugs than HTML. This means that chances that I need to resort to debugging my code are bigger, so I'm wasting more time if I use Javascript. In the above example, the quotes will cause problems when they are not properly escaped.

- Second, the above link might work on one browser but not on another, because the Document Object Model differs from one browser to another.

---

43 Whenever I see something like the above, I have to stop myself from not screaming "*NOOOOOOOooooo!!!!*". In fact, I'm screaming right now.

- Third, availability of Javascript is not obligatory for web browsers, so the link might not work at all if I happen to run another browser than whatever happened to be the favourite of the web developer.

- Fourth, even if Javascript is available on the web browser, users may disable it for security reasons.

- Fifth, bookmarking Javascript links is dodgy at best. The above example may work fine, but what if the `onClick` event calls another Javascript function that would normally be loaded by the page? This would leave us with a broken bookmark.

- But most importantly, all these reasons aside, there is a way that gives exactly the same result. A way that always works, in any and all browsers, without any of the problems mentioned above. Best of all, if you own a "HTML for beginners" manual, you will probably find it on the first page, in paragraph "How to define a hyperlink".

The following always works and can be read and maintained by anyone who has ever done anything at all in HTML:

```
<a href="x.htm">
    Click here to go to document x
</a>
```

But what if we want to open a link in another window? This can be done with the `target` attribute:

```
<a href="x.htm" target="mynewwindow">
    Click here to open document x
    (in another window)
</a>
```

If the browser is as primitive as not to support opening the site in another window, it will open it in the current one (but the link will still work). In all other cases, the above will use a new window- or reuse window `mynewwindow` when another link used it as well.

There are many more examples where plain HTML does the trick as well as Javascript. Be creative and look for them. Keep asking yourself the same question: "Is there a more standard way to do it?" More often than not, there will be a simple, standard way which will do just fine, and which will not depend on the availability of one more technology.

Keep in mind that although I have mostly addressed Javascript here, the same is true for the use of style sheets, images, Flash and whatever other fancy functionality your browser might support.

Use whatever technology you like; As long as you provide a path that will gracefully degrade the site, all functionality will remain available to all users. In contrast, *requiring* anything but the basics is bound to lock out some users.

16.3 Decide on a character encoding

After the introduction of ASCII (the American Standard Code for Information Interchange) in the year 1967, computers were suddenly able to exchange information without the need for converting the data from one character set to another.

On the World Wide Web, as long as we are dealing with static text, the regular HTML notation for accented characters goes a long way. The thought behind writing `&aacute;` or `&ccedil;` is brilliant: even in this respect, HTML permits graceful degradation. Browsers or terminals that support only ASCII can still render `&aacute;` as the letter 'a'. Also, as the HTML notation limits itself to the regular ASCII character set, it is immune to character encodings.

Unfortunately, as soon as pages are dynamically generated or if the communication between browser and server is bidirectional, converting to and from HTML notation turns out to be too much of a hassle. ASCII compliance simply isn't enough anymore, as users copy/paste content directly from their favourite word processor into their Content Management System. They won't bother to replace smart quotes (" and ") with ASCII-compatible dumb quotes ("), and the same goes for accented characters. Things are worse in a multi-lingual environment; Obviously, the ASCII character set is too limited to deal with this.

When the supported character sets of web server, browser and database differ from one another, you will be in for some more fun, as this implies converting between different character sets.

Two popular character encodings are ISO-8859 (which comes in several incarnations) and UTF-8.

UTF-8 has worked well for me. It is the default encoding for XML. It supports all characters of the Unicode character set and is widely supported across operating systems. In addition, it is ASCII compatible for diacrit-free latin text. It could work for you as well; but the downside is that you should be aware of, is that the character length is variable. As such, you need to be aware of the differences between character length and byte length when dealing with strings. If this is a problem, possibly one of the fixed length multi-byte alternatives is a better choice to you.

There are several ways to force web browsers into using the proper character encoding to display your pages. One way is to configure your web server software to do so, but this may not always be realistic (especially if you don't host your own site). Another is to add a META tag to the header section of your page:

```
<html>
    <head>
        <META http-equiv="Content-Type"
              content="text/html; charset=utf-8">
        (rest of page follows...)
```

The third way is to set it in the Content-Type in the HTTP header. In PHP, this looks as follows:

```
header('Content-Type: text/html;charset=utf-8');
```

Of course, the syntax will differ in languages other than PHP (although the header content will be the same).

Finally, make sure that your text editor can properly handle the various character encodings that you use; if it doesn't, you may end up corrupting your files- especially if you convert them from one encoding to another.

16.4 Use style sheets to control layout

Cascading style sheets are currently the most elegant way to control what your site looks like. As is the case with Javascript, it is not obligatory for browsers to support CSS. This means that you should not require CSS for your site to provide certain functionality.

If you are doing any web development at all, and you haven't learned how to work with style sheets yet, read up on them today. It will be worth the effort. The amount of HTML that you need to write will be dramatically reduced, which will improve maintainability, reduce bandwidth requirements and speed up development. In addition, style sheets will give you a lot more control over what your layout will ultimately look like.

Visit the site `http://www.csszengarden.com/` for some excellent examples of what can be done with style sheets. If you happen to have a web developer toolbar installed, try disabling the style sheets altogether: the page will gracefully degrade to readable text.

16.5 Skip the HTML/Flash/HTML cycle

An observation can be made about the progress of websites of many companies. Many times, the websites start out as static HTML, are then replaced by a fancy-looking Flash site, and finally by a database-driven website with content management system with little or no Flash. Where does this cycle come from?

My belief is that most companies start by testing the waters, wanting only something simple. The site works, and the client likes the animations and special effects that Flash is capable of, so when they upgrade, they go for a Flash site. This makes for a very fancy-looking site, but maintainability is an issue. Although the content of a Flash site does not have to be static, few web programmers are proficient both in Flash ActionScript and database-programming, so the developer of the site needs to be consulted every time that the product list of the site changes.

After some time, all these animations start to be annoying. The fact that pages are not indexed by our favourite search engine becomes an issue, as do the higher maintenance costs.

The next version of the typical site is a better-designed, database-driven HTML site that Just Works. Flash may still be used for banners and general looks of the site, but the site no longer depends on it. When we look at the websites most big companies, we see that the sites generally are not based around Flash, although some flash may be used in advertisements and for the website logo.

A problem with Flash is that it does not allow for graceful degradation. Some sites solve this by providing both an HTML version and a Flash version of the site, to be chosen by the user.

It is obvious that providing both a flash site and a non-flash site requires a duplicate effort.

Scalable Vector Graphics or SVG can be an alternative technology to Flash. As SVG is text-based (XML-based to be more specific), search engines will have no trouble indexing the pages. The text-based nature also makes SVG easier to generate, from a programmer's perspective.

However, support for it is still limited, as the W3C standard for SVG is huge. We have yet to see if SVG will catch on, or if this will cause sites to start going through HTML/SVG/HTML cycles. Personally I feel that it is more likely that SVG will find its place alongside HTML, as a way to generate and display maps and graphics, rather than to act as a replacement of HTML.

16.6 Use gracefully degradable Javascript

Javascript is a great way to enhance the responsiveness of a website when used the right way, and allows for some neat effects. It was originally intended to enhance the functionality of HTML, not to replace it. Because of this, we should treat it accordingly.

The principle of graceful degradation applies to Javascript as well. We can design a fancy site while providing a fall-back mechanism that will be used when someone with a limited browser accesses the site. The site will just work.

If Javascript is not available to set the roll-over image of a button, the button itself could still work when clicked. This ensures us our site will work on more limited browsers (such as, for example, the ones found on mobile phones).

If we want a page that is really interactive, we can't escape Javascript, or so it seems. This is however a misconception. It is always possible to submit the page to the server, allowing the server to perform any necessary interaction with the browser. Javascript can be used to prevent the need of such a round-trip.

Great examples of proper Javascript use are Google Maps and Google Mail - Javascript provides additional interactivity, but these applications will still work just fine without it.

All vital functionality of your application should at least be defined on the server, but can be duplicated in Javascript to improve responsiveness of the application. The next PHP example will work without Javascript, but will be more responsive with it. The other techniques I used are explained in the paragraphs that follow.

```php
<?php
      $submitbutton=$_POST["submitbutton"];
      $a=0;
      $b=0;
      if (strtolower($submitbutton)=="calc")
      {
            $a=$_POST["a"];
            $b=$_POST["b"];
      }
      $c=$a+$b;
?><html><head><title>test</title>
<script language="javascript"><!--
    function calcval(document)
    {
        var a=document.form.a.value;
        var b=document.form.b.value;
        var c=a+b;
        result=document.getElementById("result");
        result.innerHTML=c;
        return false; // do not submit the form
    }
  // --></script>
  </head>
  <body>
    <form name="form" id="form"
          method="post" action="">
      Enter value A:
      <input type="text"
              name="a" id="a" value="<?=$a?>">
      <br>Enter value B:
      <input type="text"
              name="b" id="b" value="<?=$b?>">
      <br>Sum of A+B=
      <div id="result"><?=$c?></div>
      <input type="submit"
              name="submitbutton"
              value="calc"
              onclick="returncalcval(document);">
    </form>
  </body>
</html>
```

16.7 Let web pages post to themselves

The first means of server-side processing of data were CGI scripts. Web languages have come a long way since then, although most of them nowadays are based on the same principles. ASP, PHP and JSP are strikingly similar. This is logical, because in the end, they all work on the same platform: A standardized web browser and a server that serves up the pages for it.

In the example in the previous paragraph, you will see that the page posts to itself. For creating (semi) interactive applications, I find this is a practice that works very well. Not only does it allow us to treat a web page as a complete, stand-alone module in a single file, it also makes it easy to make pages that refill themselves after a post action, rather than requiring an additional development effort to make a page saying "You made this-and-that mistake on the form. Please click back and try again."

If we let a form post to itself, we make it much easier to redisplay the form along with all data that was entered in it, and along with error messages relevant to that data[44]. This also allows us to use the same form file to enter either new data or to edit existing data.

By having a form post to itself, we raise the assumption that the browser always stays on the same page, unless redirected by specific action. Redirecting is done by sending a HTTP redirect. In PHP this would be something along the lines of

```
header("Location: http://www.google.com");
```

---

44 Also see page 161.

This statement is executed on the server side, before any data is sent to the browser. All web programming platforms allow sending headers. Redirecting the browser to another page by means of a Location header is present and supported by all browsers, as it has been part of the HTTP standard since the beginning to accommodate for moved pages. Not a single line of Javascript is needed to redirect the browser. Should we want to 'repost' variables from our current page to the other one, we can do so by either passing them in the URL of the header statement, or by means of session variables.

16.8 Validate and compute on the server

As we have seen from the former example, it is possible to create a web page that works either with or without Javascript.

A drawback that is very visible from that example, is that some code is duplicated: the calculation code (or business logic, if you will) is present both on the client (as Javascript) and on the server (in this case, as PHP). In our search for the Holy Grail of perfect code, this is not acceptable, because doubling the amount of code doubles the risk of bugs. In addition, it will cost us extra time to implement both server-code and client-code, which we might not have.

Given the choice to either give up Javascript or server-side code, the choice is clear. If we want to have any control over the validity of data that the server needs to write to the database, we need to at least perform checks on the server side. After all, if someone decides to bypass checks on the client by disabling Javascript, we're done for. The result of this policy is that we'll see our applications gain robustness and use less Javascript. This is a pity, because Javascript is a very useful addition to web programming.

When it comes to validating input, it probably makes most sense to have the server generate some Javascript for it. Easily checked, generic conditions can be checked on the browser: characters accepted, field length, field format, entering data in required fields. This will prevent most round trips to the server. By leaving specific validations to the server, not only will you have more control over the final validations than Javascript can give you, but you will also prevent the browser from ever needing to directly access the database, making for better separation of presentation, business logic and data layer.

16.9 Use one form called form

As the Great Browser Wars started between Netscape and Microsoft, each of them invented their own flavour of Javascript, each with their own Document Object Model. Unfortunately, these two object models are not compatible with each other. As a result, Javascript code that is specifically aimed at the Document Object Model of one browser will not properly work in the other.

There is however one trick that will solve the biggest incompatibility, opening the door to use some Javascript here and there. In the old Netscape browser, it was only possible to design pages that had a single submittable form. Internet Explorer, in the meantime, allowed multiple forms, each with a different name. You could have a form called `form1`, and another one called `form2`. When in Explorer we want to access the value of a field in the first form, we write

```
document.form1.fieldname.value
```

whereas in the old Netscape browsers (and all their derivatives, including Firefox) we would write

```
document.form.fieldname.value
```

By the way, the latter is officially the correct way, according to the World Wide Web Consortium. Strange enough, as a member of the W3C, Microsoft didn't always follow the official W3C standards in their browser.

We can solve this incompatibility by using only a single form and naming it `form`. In Explorer, this will make the form accessible by its name `form`, so accessing fields on the form looks like this:

```
document.form.fieldname.value
```

which is, surprisingly, equal to the name of the form object in all Netscape derivatives. Should it be necessary to post to multiple different locations, a `Location` header can pass the values to those locations, instead of a form.

16.10 Name and ID HTML fields equally

When you give fields an ID that is equal to their name, any Javascript-enabled browser will be able to access them as document elements using the getElementById function. Be aware that the function name getElementById is case sensitive.

```html
<html><head><title>Dynamic field filler</title>
<script language="Javascript"><!--
function docalc(document)
{
    // Fill fields with their field number
    // (using dynamically generated field names)
    for (i=1;i<=1000;i++)
    {
        field=document.getElementById("field"+i);
        field.value=i;
    }
    return false; // do not submit
}
// --></script>
</head>
<body>
<form name="form" id="form" method="post" action="">
  <?php
      for ($i=1;$i<=1000;$i++) {
          /* dynamically generate 1000 fields
              (in this case, using PHP) */
  ?><input name="field<?=$i?>" id="field<?=$i?>"
      type="text" value="">
  <?  }
  ?><input type="submit"
        name="submitbutton" value="calc"
        onclick="return docalc(document);">
</form></body>
</html>
```

16.11 Use DIVs to allow dynamic behaviour

Although `DIV` tags don't do much by themselves, they are very useful placeholders to group together page elements. Preparing your pages with `DIV` tags is a great way to prepare your pages for interactive behaviour. Using the `getElementById` function, it is then possible to access `DIV`s by their ID and set their `innerHTML` property to a snippet of HTML, after the page has already been rendered.

Using `DIV` tags in combination with `getElementById` allows for mighty interactivity, and allows us to control elements that are not controllable in any other way.

Using `DIV` tags in combination with CSS stylesheets allows overlapping layers on a page, which is very useful for things such as pop-up date pickers. Unlike old-fashioned Netscape layers, `DIV` tags are cross-browser compatible.

The example on page 331 already showed a hint of how `DIV` tags may be used to dynamically alter web pages after they have been loaded.

The example on the next page just shows the part that dynamically alters the page after loading.

```html
<html>
  <head>
    <title>
        Change page after rendering
    </title>
    <script language="javascript"><!--

    function calcval(document)
    {
      result=document.getElementById("result");
      result.innerHTML="Hello world!";
      return false;
    }

    // --></script>
  </head>
  <body>
    <form name="form" method="post" action="">
    <div id="result">Hi there</div>
    <input type="submit"
          name="submitbutton" value="calc"
          onclick="return calcval(document);">
    </form>
  </body>
</html>
```

The `innerHTML` property is read-write, so it is possible to read the `innerHTML` of an element, alter it and write it back.

One should keep in mind that although it is a very powerful technique, altering the `innerHTML` of an element is not necessarily the prettiest way to do things. It has a few downsides: It alters the in-memory HTML of the page, whereas "view source" in the average browser only shows the source of the page as it looked when the page was loaded.

You can overcome this problem by installing a developer toolbar for your browser. If such a toolbar is not available for your browser, a workaround is to inspect the contents of the `DIV` by adding a line of Javascript to our code, for example:

```
alert(document.getElementById("mydivid").innerHTML);
```

This will access the currently active HTML contents of the DIV with ID `mydivid`, instead of the contents as they were when the page was being loaded.

You can use `elements=getElementsByTagName("div");` to access all DIVs on your page (or other tags, depending on the parameter). Loop through the array elements to process them one at a time.

16.12 Avoid frames

To starting web developers, frames seem like an interesting idea. They allow you to reload part of a page, while keeping the rest of the site on screen. However, the drawbacks are considerable:

- Passing data between frames is relatively tricky, making it likely that using frames also introduces a Javascript dependency.

- To the user, bookmarking pages no longer works properly.

- Search engines have trouble with them.

- Frames potentially lock you into a static design.

- Frames make your site less accessible to visually impaired people.

- When one frame is loaded, another may not yet be. As a result, if you use Javascript, it needs to perform a lot of extra checks just to check if the frame is already there.

If you are using frames for layout purposes, you really should be using style sheets instead. These will give you a lot more flexibility than frames. If you absolutely require an element that can individually post and reload its own contents, `iframe` elements are for you; they can act almost identical to frames, but you'll have much more control over their positioning by using style sheets. The next paragraph deals with the last reason to use frames.

16.13 Prevent unnecessary reloads

In the past, some people used frames to make web pages more responsive. A website would be visible in one frame, and another, hidden frame would act as data transfer area.

Whenever a certain event occurred (such as selecting an item from a drop-down box), the web page would trigger a server request to load some data into the hidden frame. After this, the `onLoad` event of the hidden frame would update part of the content of the visible page, which had remained unchanged while the frame was being loaded.

Imagine a search engine page; The user can enter a query and click submit. Now we will add some Javascript and a hidden frame. If Javascript is disabled, we will maintain the existing behaviour. However, if Javascript is available, we will let each keystroke perform a submit to the server, loading the very same search engine page in a hidden frame. After loading the page in the hidden frame, its `onLoad` event will update the results in the original page. With a minimum of extra code, we have accomplished the following:

- If the user does have Javascript, the web page will suddenly be highly interactive.

- All the code for the page is still centralized within that one page.

- The page does not require Javascript; it is still fully functional to users that do not have Javascript or that have disabled it.

As mentioned, originally this technique was implemented with a hidden frame; For backwards compatibility with old browsers, it still could be implemented in this manner.

However, there's been a new kid in town for a few years. It is the XMLHttpRequest which works pretty much in the same manner as the hidden frame, but a hidden frame is no longer required.

Being acknowledged by the World Wide Web Consortium, using the XMLHttpRequest object is now the recommended way of creating highly interactive web applications.

The benefit of using XMLHttpRequest is probably most visible when only a small snippet of a page needs to be updated. For instance, when we have a full, one-year calendar on screen and we click a single day cell, we can avoid the browser to reload and rendering a rather heavy page. Instead, only the contents of a single table cell needs to be loaded; this is obviously a much lighter operation.

Regardless of the availability of Javascript or XMLHttpRequest, it is still a good idea to prevent round-trips to the server in other ways. For instance, if a form needs to be filled in, it would be horrible to receive only one error message at a time if the form contains ten errors. If we need to fill in a weekly time sheet and we are forced to submit one day at a time, this will require us to reload the form several times. Doesn't it make more sense to submit several days at once?

16.14 Avoid using the userAgent string

Some websites that rely heavily on Javascript, will perform browser detection by means of the userAgent string and block any browser that doesn't happen to be the favourite of the developer. Code that uses the userAgent string typically looks something like the following:

```
if (navigator.userAgent.indexOf('IE') == -1)
{
      document.write("We only support IE");
}
else
{
      document.write("Welcome to our page");
}
```

As `document.write()` works best before the page has finished loading, a server-side solution would make more sense; but the server has no business interfering with Javascript.

Apart from the fact that the above example shows that the site introduces a Javascript dependency to function, it is blocking browsers that might be perfectly capable of rendering the site. Also, there is no guarantee that the next version of IE won't be rebranded, breaking the site.

But most of all, many modern browsers allow their users to set the userAgent string to whatever they please. This makes using the userAgent string an unreliable mechanism to detect which browser is accessing your site.

By using the userAgent string, our code has to make assumptions about whether certain features of Javascript are available or not by the browser in which the code is running. Instead of making such assumptions based on an unreliable mechanism, why not simply figure out if certain features are supported? In most cases, it is possible to sniff for the existence of special features, for example:

```
function getHTML(iframeEdit)
{
    /* Copy HTML from an IFRAME to a
       hidden html field. */
    var explorer=true;
    var moz=true;
    // Try reading the IE way first
    try {
        var framedoc=iframeEdit.document;
        return framedoc.body.innerHTML;
    } catch (e) {
        explorer=false;
    }

    // okay, let's try the Moz way
    try {
        var framedoc=
         iframeEdit.contentWindow.document;
        return framedoc.body.innerHTML;
    } catch (e) {
        moz=false;
    }
    alert('Unsupported browser');
}
```

Even though this code is still targeted at a few key browsers, it allows any Javascript-enabled browser to take a shot at rendering the page, so at least it checks for their capabilities instead of assuming that things won't work by the userAgent string. Users will only be faced with an error message if their browser *really* doesn't support the given functionality, in which case they still might be provided a non-Javascript alternative.

Chapter 17

The future of programming tools

Programming tools nowadays are a lot better than they used to be. We now have shiny Integrated Development Environments in which we can draw user interfaces by dragging and dropping buttons and such, as well as better programming languages, design tools, process control tools, and so on.

But they are still a far cry from what they could become. The following paragraphs deal with a few realistic steps that could be taken to improve the way we build information systems.

17.1 Variable code layout

There have been long discussions about where to put brackets-at the end of the line or on a line of themselves? Using a separate line for just a bracket is a waste of space; Putting the bracket at the end of the line makes it less clear which bracket is the closing bracket. If you are a Python programmer, this is probably a non-issue to you. But for many other languages, why not have an IDE that places the brackets where we prefer them, rather than where the last programmer left them?

Some Integrated Development Environments already have layout engines for pretty-printing the code. But we can take this a step further. There are programmers that prefer writing single-exit code, and programmers that prefer to write early-exit code. As the structure of code is identical regardless of the actual code written, it should be possible to let editors display code in either form.

If some programmers prefer viewing code in early-exit notation, and other programmers in single-exit notation, so much the better: viewing code in different ways will reveal different types of errors.

Of course this is relatively complex to build, as code editors would need go a few steps further than syntax highlighting. They would need to analyze the structure of the code.

17.2 Integrated PSD generation

It would be even better to have our editors view Program Structure Diagrams instead of a pure textual representation of our code. Although software exists to create or display Program Structure Diagrams, it involves either a rather elaborate process to manually draw the diagrams, or creates diagrams statically based on a source listing. At present, no truly integrated solution exists.

One obstacle in adapting PSD-editors seems to be the required screen width. This could be addressed by applying the concept of folding editors horizontally. I would like to see a type of folding editor which requires little or no change from our usual way of writing code, but which draws up code as a Program Structure Diagram, as the code is being written.

With such an editor, branches of an IF statement would be next to each other rather than one following the other. This would help us give strong visual clues about the structure of our code.

As such, PSD-viewing editors would help programmers write beautifully structured code, rather than distracting them with the single-exit vs. multiple-exits flame war.

17.3 Design Warnings

Our current programming systems allow us to create the most disgusting systems without ever receiving a warning that the design of our system isn't solid. More often than not this results in an unmaintainable mess.

A good start would be to have programming tools that warn us when we present them with potentially flawed code such as the following:

```
int a(object object1)
{
    int x=object1.getobject2.getvalue();
    return x;
}
```

The above lacks checks for `null` values. There is no reason why this should compile without warnings. Likewise, it would be great if our compilers would warn us of badly structured code, overly long functions, functions with side effects, hard-coded values, and so on. If we write such code and we *know* it is correct, we could tell the compiler so by including meta-information in comments. This idea is not new; SPARK-ADA does just this. Clearly, some progress seems to be on its way in this area, but there is still a long way to go.

In the design of data(base) structures, too, there is a lot left to be desired; it is too easy to create data structures that aren't normalized, requiring a lot more code to deal with them. Unfortunately, data structures usually deal with the semantics rather than syntax, which makes it much harder to warn their designers about bad form.

17.4 Automatically rewriting code

There are quite a few techniques mentioned in this book that show how to improve written code. Based on these techniques, we can manually refactor code, and soon will find that it is a rather repetitive, mechanical job- possibly something that a computer could help us with.

Some automatic refactoring capabilities have made their way into mainstream software: tools already exist to extract code into functions, or to help us rename variables by following the semantics of a program, rather than by doing a crude search and replace. However, more extreme refactoring of the actual structure of the code should be possible as well.

It is easy to envision a code editor with a menu option 'Restructure current function' that would reduce extent, prevent overriding return values, put code in the most efficient order, and generally simplify the code.

Extent analysis combined with syntax-highlighting could indicate if variables are either read or written anywhere else in the remainder of the function, or if variables are being used without being verified first. This would make certain classes of bugs much more obvious.

17.5 Tools that help us design for change

Despite all wizards that may exist to help us creating the framework of our first program, when it comes to changing our code, we are mostly on our own. What's worse, our programming environments never warn us when we were writing code that will be hard to maintain.

In designing databases and data structures we're also pretty much on our own, even more so when we need to alter their structure: Until now, we're stuck manually writing our own data migration modules.

It is possible to think of a better data definition language that has a stronger basis in information analysis than our current SQL Data Definition Language. By providing a bit more semantic information, it should be possible to create databases that not only perform better (because no unnecessary normalization is going on), but that will also be easier to maintain and upgrade.

The following is an incomplete example of what a data structure definition in such a language could look like. For those who have read the first chapters of this text, it should look familiar. It is a case of object-oriented programming meets SQL meets information-analysis.

```
database invoice
#include client
each shortstring is "varchar(255)"
each date is "date"
each percentage is "integer"
each number is "number"


/* only the text between quotes above is DBMS-
dependent. */

each currency_code is shortstring
each conversion_rate is number
each entity_being_paid is commonobject

each currency is commonobject /* inheritance,
                                 polymorphism */
has 1..1 currency_code       /* properties */
has 1..1 conversion_rate
each currency_code has 1..1 currency
each conversion_rate has 0..many currency
each client has 0..many invoice
each invoice has 1..1 client
```

The above snippet already deals with primary keys, foreign keys, required fields and unique constraints. It is possible to translate the above into SQL DDL without much trouble; we could write a script to automate this.

In addition, information about the data structure of the database could be stored in the database itself, for the purpose of generating migration scripts.

Consider the last two statements of the above example:

```
each client has 0..many invoice
each invoice has 1..1 client
```

If a client can have several invoices, but an invoice has only 1 client, it makes sense for a database to have one table of invoices containing a field with the foreign key for a client, whereas client data (being a complex data structure) would be contained by another table.

If in a traditional system we would want to assign multiple clients to a single invoice, this would require restructuring the database. A single foreign key field in the invoice table wouldn't be enough anymore. Instead, we'd have to create a new table specifically aimed at relating clients to invoices, and then manually create a data migration script.

However, in our imaginary language, all we have to do is to change the last line to

```
each invoice has 1..many client
```

and we're done. As the database contains all meta-data needed to describe its own structure, the database migration script that migrates the existing data from a 1-to-1 relation to a 1-to-many relation can be completely generated. The same also applies, for example, to altering the data type of percentages from integer to floating-point. We could limit ourselves to specifying this once, in the beginning of the file, and the system would be able to take care of migrating data and the rest.

Of course, in an environment like this, it would no longer be possible to access data by directly performing SQL on the database, because it would not be known which tables or fields would exist in it at any given moment.

Instead, an interface would be generated that would allow us to access, for instance, all clients belonging to an invoice. Beneath the surface of the system, tables and columns would still exist, but in a manner that is as sparingly normalized as possible, allowing for maximum performance.

The above example unfortunately only deals with the information analysis of a system, not with the code that interacts with it. Perhaps at some point in the future, both database structure and the code that accesses it can be automatically upgraded to reflect design changes. Until then, we should keep ourselves trained to think of systems in such a way that they support many-to-many relationships, to keep our databases easily upgradeable.

17.6 Parallel programming

Multi-core processors are now a reality. It can be expected that this will bring some great performance benefits. From a software perspective, however, it also means added complexity. One of the reasons parallel programming is so hard, is that it greatly increases the number of states that our program can have at any given moment. For this reason, for the stability of your software, it would be recommendable to keep the number of concurrent processes in your program to a minimum, when possible.

Where single-thread debugging tools allow you to single-step your code and get to the root cause of the problem, this approach does not work for parallel code. For this reason too, avoiding concurrency is best.

But the current state of hardware dictates otherwise. If we are to use our new hardware to its fullest potential, we have to learn how to use it.

Our current programming languages allow creating threads, processes and semaphores in one way or another. But there is little support to ensure bug-free concurrent operation, and unless we explicitly write parallel code, our programs won't run any faster on multi-core processors than they do on single-core.

Hopes are that compiler designers will come up with a way to perform automatic parallelization (especially of loops), so that we can keep writing code as before. It is a good idea to prevent loop iterations to depend on the previous iteration, as this makes it more likely for new compilers to be able to automatically parallelize our loops. Until compiler designers figure out how to do this, extending languages with a `map` statement such as exists in Perl may provide a realistic alternative.

Chapter 18

General considerations

We are approaching the end of this book, so I'm left with a few general, but important considerations to give you.

18.1 Be aware of existing standards

Rather than reinventing the wheel for frequently occurring problems, it pays off to be familiar with extending standards. This will increase the chances that your software will be able to interoperate with other software. To name a few:

Standard code	Description
ISO 3166	Country codes
ISO 639	Language codes (obsolete)
ISO 8601	Date/time standard (includes week numbering)
ISO 4127	Currency codes
ISO/IEC 11578:1996	Universally Unique Identifiers

Protocols will often be identified with an RFC number:

Standard code	Description
RFC 821/2821	Simple Mail Transfer Protocol
RFC 3501	Internet Message Access Protocol
RFC 959	File Transfer Protocol
RFC 2616	HyperText Transfer Protocol

Finally, there are standards telling us how to do our jobs:

Standard code	Description
ISO 9000	Quality management standard
ISO/IEC 27001	Security standard

18.2 Know the basic stuff

By getting familiar with common data structures and algorithms, we will be able to make better choices about how to solve problems.

You should be intimately familiar with data structures such as linked lists, stacks, circular lists, binary trees, ternary trees and hash tables. You should be familiar with recursion, as it can greatly increase the simplicity and maintainability of your code.

You should be intimately familiar with bubble sort (even if for no other reason than to avoid it) and quick sort, and be aware that other sorting methods exist that may be more suitable in specific circumstances. You should be able to work in binary and hexadecimal numeral systems.

It pays off to read the occasional paper and technical specification documents on specific subjects, as it will help you solve problems that you would otherwise not have a solution for.

18.3 Know your environment

By having intimate knowledge of the environment that you're programming in, it is possible to come up with better solutions. Usually, this means having some knowledge on a deeper level than the level that we're working on: If we are programming in Java, it helps to know a few things about the virtual machine that is running our code; if we are programming in C, it helps to know a thing or two about compiler construction and assembly language; if we are programming in assembly, it helps to know a few things about the hardware that we are working on.

18.4 Learn how to build it yourself

One of the best ways to learn about the environment that you are working in, is to roll your own.

For instance, by creating your own programming language, you will end up with a truckload of knowledge about how programming languages work in general. This understanding will make you a better programmer.

Of course, although it is a useful exercise to build things yourself, it does not mean that you always have to build your own solution to problems that have been solved long ago.

18.5 First make it work, then make it great

One way to solve problems is to start by building something that works, then improving on it until it is great. When a program adds value, it is worth money; by keeping things simple at first, it will be possible to deliver a program very soon. This program may not be ideal and it may not be pretty, but it will solve a problem. From that point on, the program will be able to pay for itself.

Before you start, however, try to have a vision of what the 'finished' version of the program should be like. This will help you to keep the program flexible enough to reach that vision, while it is being developed.

To the client, a benefit of this approach is that the program will not be overpaid; it will only be developed for as long as it adds value.

18.6 No assumptions

Do not make assumptions, but make sure; making assumptions is the same as guessing.

We do not want to guess if our client wants a feature, we want to make sure; otherwise we end up spending time on building features that the client didn't ask for.

We do not want to make assumptions about the validity of the input of our users and cause a huge security leak.

We do not want to make assumptions about the operating system used by our clients, or the amount of free memory they have, or the amount of disk space. If instead of assuming, we make sure, this will allow us to grow better software.

18.7 Remember to have a good time

Last but not least, remember to have a good time. Only when you are feeling at your best, you will be working at your best. So take care of yourself, eat well, take your time to relax, and have some fun once in a while!

Good luck!

Alphabetical Index

www.ingramcontent.com/pod-product-compliance
Lightning Source LLC
Chambersburg PA
CBHW051222050326
40689CB00007B/770